A SHORT HISTORY OF THEATREWORKS
(1979- 1994)

Paul Michael Davies

Detail from Mirka Mora's Mosaic on St. Kilda Beach (1997)

This book is copyright. Apart from any fair dealing for the purpose of private study, research or review, as permitted under the Copyright Act, no part may be reproduced by any process without written permission. Inquiries concerning publication, translation or recording rights should be addressed to the author.

© The moral right of the author has been asserted.

Cover Design by Tabitha Davies

First Edition
Gondwana Press
November 2020
Suffolk Park NSW 2481

Bringing the World
Back Together

CONTENTS

Assembled TheatreWorkers on the payroll as at 30th June 1984 Universal Theatre Fitzroy (the set for *Dee Jay View*)

TheatreWorks

1979	5
1980	9
1981	13
1882	23
1983	33
1984	41
1985	49
1986	57
1987	63
1988	69
1989	75
1990	83
1991	89

The Really Moving Theatre Company

1992	91
1994	95

Why TheatreWorks?	97
Caz Howard (1952 – 1990)	129
Other Books by Paul Davies	131
Author	133

1979

Within the Victorian College of the Arts the prospective TheatreWorks ensemble (and other students in the same year), were known collectively as 'Company '80' – which derived from their year of graduation at the end of 1980. One play that identified the TheatreWorks founding members as a group sharing similar cultural and socio-political aspirations was *Fanshen* by David Hare

FANSHEN (early 1979)

Location: Grant Street Theatre, Victorian College of the Arts
Script: David Hare
Cast: Susie Fraser, Hannie Rayson, Amanda Ma, Peter Sommerfeld, Peter Finlay, Caz Howard, Nicki Compton, Christof Gregory.

TheatreWorks five founding members fill the cast of *Fanshen*
(L – R) Susie Fraser, Nicki Compton, Hannie Rayson, Christof Gregory, Amanda Ma, Peter Sommerfeld, Peter Finlay, Caz Howard.

David Hare's play about the struggle of a group of peasants in a small village dealing with the arrival of Maoism in 1949 was not officially a TheatreWorks production since the company didn't exist yet. However, this contemporary play, with its minimal staging and Brechtian undertow, drew together all the original TheatreWorks cohort for the first time. The play's legacy lived on in the 'Chairman Mao' exercise routine which preceded most TheatreWorks warm-ups for years afterwards (and which Caz Howard in particular insisted on doing).

Susie Fraser:
"*Fanshen.* That was another defining moment. Some people did Tennessee Williams and we did *Fanshen* [laughs]. That set us apart. It was huge transcripts based on a lot of doco material from the Chinese cultural revolution and it wasn't about practicing your emotive acting it was more Brechtian and group work and ensemble."[1]

JANUARY 1979

EXITS **(released 1980)**

Location:	National Theatre, St. Kilda, various streets, pubs, beaches, dumps and other found locations around Melbourne, includes documentary footage of the Whitlam sacking and associated demonstrations.
Script:	Paul Davies
Direction:	Pat Laughren, Caz Howard, Paul Davies
Cast:	Caz Howard, Paul Davies, Robert Antoniades, Pat Laughren, Eric Beach, Mary Anne Grey.

---

[1] Susie Fraser Personal Interview, St. Kilda 15/2/2010

(camera Paul Cavell)

Exits (1979) Paul Davies and co-director Pat Laughren
on location beside a wall found in Collingwood, Melbourne

Again, although not officially a TheatreWorks production, the short feature film *Exits* (an experimental docu-drama set against the sacking of the Whitlam Labour Government four years earlier), brought together Caz Howard and Paul Davies in their first collaboration, and it was a tram ride home together after the final editing session for the film, that the real life incident which inspired the *Tram Show* took place. Significantly, being essentially a 'no-budget' film, *Exits* was shot entirely on location, encouraging the idea in the participants that performance could and did happen anywhere; that performance space could be defined and mapped out by a film crew, and framed by a narrative, and that an absence of constructed elements enhanced authenticity of this ever shifting relationship between fiction and reality.

APRIL 7 – 11, 1979

FEFU AND HER FRIENDS

Location:	A large mansion in Elwood, Melbourne
Script:	Marina Irene Fornes
Direction:	Ros Horin
Design	Peter Sommerfeld
Cast:	Caz Howard (Fefu) Susie Fraser (Julia) Hannie Rayson (Emma), Amanda Ma (Sue), Amanda Pile (Cecilia) Lunne ? (Cindy) Anne Tuohy (Christina) Cathy Lynch (Paula)

(photo: *Theatre Australia* 1979)
Fefu and Her Friends (Maria Irene Fornés 1977)
VCA Production directed by Ros Horin April, 1979.
L-R: Caz Howard (back), Cathrine Lynch, Amanda Pile,
Amanda Ma, Lynn Howard, Hannie Rayson.

A third production at the Victorian College for the Arts in which the emerging TheatreWorks core group (specifically the women: Susie Fraser, Caz Howard and Hannie Rayson) took part, was Marina Irene Fornes' 1977 play, *Fefu And Her Friends*. Although set in the roaring 20s, this play was hot off the press and like Hannie Rayson's second play *Mary*, had a cast consisting exclusively of women. Interestingly, in a staging strategy that would presage the one adopted for *Living Rooms*, this production of *Fefu* was located in a large house in Tennyson Street in the bayside suburb of Elwood. The house was being rented by several other students at the VCA Acts or 'Parts' of the play that take place in the Living Room, the Study, Kitchen were re-enacted in the equivalent rooms of the found building.

DECEMBER 1979

Entry from Peter Finlay's Journal for Monday 11th December 1979:
> About 11.30 at Suzie Fraser's place for a Burwood meeting all day. Talking aims and methods and arranged appointments to meet Chris Walsh [Victorian Ministry for the Arts] and Roz Bower…About mid-afternoon Suzie consulted the I-Ching as we struggled for a name for the group. It was the hexagram No.9 – "The taming power of the Small." We decided to call ourselves "TheatreWorks".

1980

TheatreWorks founding members
(L-R) Susie Fraser, Peter Finlay, Hannie Rayson, (Chi) Caz Howard, Peter Sommerfeld

In their final year at the VCA the emerging TheatreWorks core group produced two plays, the first by Hannie Rayson. Essentially, this is where the company formally starts. In fact *Please Return To Sender* was specifically designed to tour the eastern suburbs as a scouting exercise for a potential move out there the following year.

MAY 1980

PLEASE RETURN TO SENDER

Location: Grant St. Theatre foyer, Victorian College of the Arts, plus various halls and community centres in the eastern suburbs including Burwood State College, Box Hill Community Centre, Rusden State College, Spastic Society Glen Waverley Centre Hall, Camberwell Civic Theatrette, The Hall Nunawading, Nunawading Community Centre, Syndal Hall.
Script: Hannie Rayson
Direction: Cathy Mueller

Assistant Director: Andrea Lemon
Technical Direction: Tony Kishawi
Musical Direction: Betty Greenbaum
Design: Peter Sommerfeld
Cast: Caz Howard, Susie Fraser, Tony Kishawi, Chrissie Best, Peter Finlay, Richard Vinycomb, Hannie Rayson, Mary Sitarenos, Peter Sommerfeld
Synopsis: The trials and tribulations of a postman, Marty Pankston, who suddenly finds himself unplanned and pregnant.

Cast and Crew of *Please Return To Sender* (VCA 1980)
L – R Back Row: Cathy Mueller (director) Caz Howard, Susie Fraser, Tony Kishawi, Andrea Lemon (assistant director)
Front Row: Chrissie Best, Peter Finlay, Richard Vinycomb, Hannie Rayson, Mary Sitarenos

The set for *Please Return to Sender* was a scaffolding construction designed to take the play into various Eastern Suburban locations, including Burwood State College, Box Hill Community Centre, Rusden State College, the Spastic Society, Glen Waverly Centre Hall, Camberwell Civic Theatrette, the hall Nunawading, Nunawading Community Centre, and Syndal Hall. Mobility is clearly endemic in the company's work from this first production: the idea of moving out, taking theatre into the suburbs where it had never been before, at least in a 'professional' sense. Because this was not seen as extension or addition to the amateur dramatic society 'movement' the 'little theatre' tradition that peppers many small towns and regions.

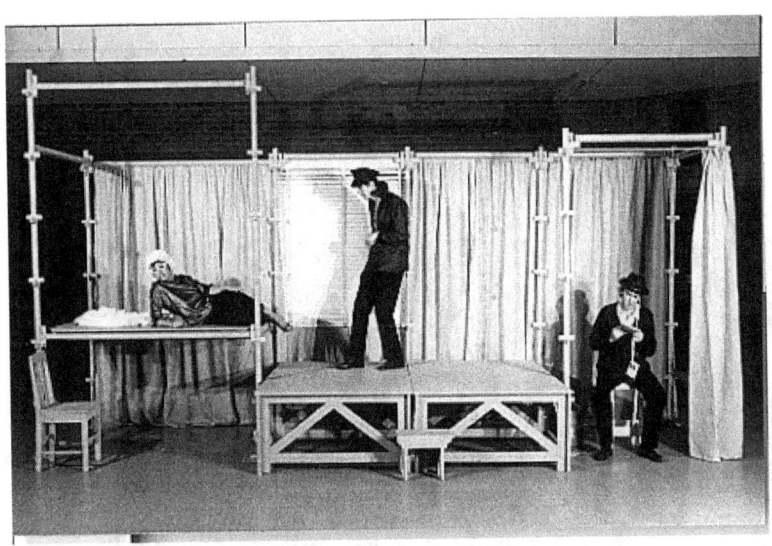

On tour with *Please Return To Sender*
L – R   Susie Fraser, Peter Finlay, Peter Sommerfeld,

Hannie Rayson:
> We had scaffolding that framed a stage and we took that on tour around various church halls. A reverend told me, after one performance as we were washing up the cups, that 'I've never enjoyed anything so much that I've disagreed with so much.' What he meant was the message in the play that abortion was an option. Stephen Lusher in 1978 had mooted in parliament that abortion should be put on the agenda and members should have a conscience vote. That was the inciting incident. So I had a man get pregnant (in one testicle). It must've been at the height of my feminism."

Because of Peter Sommerfeld's connection with Burwood State College (as an art lecturer there) TheatreWorks first official base was a small office on the campus. But it also gave the new company access to the nearby Phoenix Theatre and as a way of announcing themselves as the new company in residence, TheatreWorks staged their first production outside of the VCA.

NOVEMBER   13 – 23RD 1980

DEE JAY VIEW — **25 years of Rock and Roll in Australia**
Location: Phoenix Theatre, Burwood State College
Script: Peter Sommerfeld
Direction: Richard Murphet
Design: Peter Sommerfeld
Cast: Peter Finlay Amanda Ma, Susie Fraser, Caz Howard, Hannie Rayson, Steve Scully, Tony Kishawi
Admission: $3/$2

Dee Jay View
L – R   Top: Peter Finlay Amanda Ma, Susie Fraser,
Middle: Caz Howard, , Hannie Rayson, Steve Scully,
Front: Peter Sommerfeld Tony Kishawi

Originally called *"The Rocky History Show"*, *Dee Jay View* was written by Peter Sommerfeld and described as a "collage of dialogue/conversations/visuals and songs based on the lives of eight 'original teenagers' – the people who first heard rock and roll in 1956 at the age of 15, and who now find they are 40. It's the story of their times." [2]

---

[2] Press Release for DJ View (first production) TheatreWorks Archive Box #1

1981

With a small grant, essentially seed funding from the Victorian Ministry for the Arts, TheatreWorks was legally incorporated on 22nd February 1981 as "The Eastern Suburbs Community Theatre Company", a non profit organisation run by a board of directors and limited by guarantee.

From a pitch document to funding bodies for the 1981 programme:

> "TheatreWorks is a group that is committed to social change but is not aligned to any particular political philosophy. We are primarily artists who believe in theatre as a positive force in our society. " [3]

L- R Caz Howard, Jill Warne (Admin) and Suzi Fraser
Hard at work applying for grants

---

[3] TheatreWorks Archive, Company Papers Box 16, Fryer Library Brisbane)

APRIL – DECEMBER 1981

THE GO ANYWHERE (within reason) SHOW (70+ performances)

Locations: Camping Grounds, Factories, Festivals, Special Schools, Sheltered Workshops, Community Centres, Halls, Winlaton (girls remand centre) Burwood Drop-In centre for Elderly Citizens, Mt. Waverly Youth Centre, Alkira Training Centre, Fountain Gate Shopping Centre, Monash University, Camberwell Civic Centre and Fairlea women's prison.

Script: (Peter Finlay, Hannie Rayson with input from director and cast)

Length: 30 minutes

Direction: Robin Laurie

Design: Peter Sommerfeld, Tony Kishawi

Cast: Peter Finlay, Caz Howard, Susie Fraser, Tony Kishawi, Hannie Rayson

The Go Anywhere Show
Cast and crew have tent will travel
L-R   Top: Peter Finlay (Dick Dickens) Caz Howard (Dolly Dickens), Susie Fraser, (Desdemona Dickens)
Bottom: Tony Kishawi (Darryl Dickens) Robin Laurie (director) Hannie Rayson (Daphne Dickens)

Having struggled with touring the somewhat clunky scaffolding and rostra set designed for *Please Return To Sender*, TheatreWorks found a much more transportable theatre/prop in the form of a tent; especially in the idea that it could 'define' a stage area, as well as conceal props and characters. It was also seen as an ideal icon for a 'location' play that satirised an suburban family's hopeless, homeless, jobless predicament. In this sense the subject matter and the theatre-deprived circumstances of the company making it worked in tandem. in The Australian economy underwent a downturn in the early 1980s and TheatreWorks response was a play about keeping up appearances, hiding the inevitable, radiating eternal optimism, and all the while pretending, in the face of adversity that everything was okay. In the venerable tradition of all tent shows *The Go Anywhere Show* could be done ... well virtually anywhere (within reason). It was an important first step as TheatreWorks pushed further into its chosen suburban heartland, looking for places to colonise theatrically. *The Go Anywhere Show* offered "comedy, audience participation, music plus a little bit of wisdom"[4]

---

[4] TheatreWorks Archive, Newsletters & Annual Reports, Fryer Library Brisbane)

Hannie Rayson and Tony Kishawi

Peter Finlay:
> " We came up with the idea camping at Wilson's Prom. [a national park on the Victorian Coast]. Hannie and I did a lot of the writing for it. A lot of the dialogue was hers. There were also impros [improvisations] built into it. Such as the setting up the deck chair lahzi[5] which effectively defined the playing space. Robin Laurie was really interested in *Commedia della'arte*. So there was a lot of physical business built into it."

---

[5] A 'lahzi' was a slang word of indeterminate spelling, in currency at the VCA at that time (1980s) which derived from the clowning traditions of the *Commedia della'arte*. It referred to a sequence of purely physical action in which usually some kind of pratfall or non-verbal transaction took place between the characters, often quite detailed subject to improvisation in its execution.

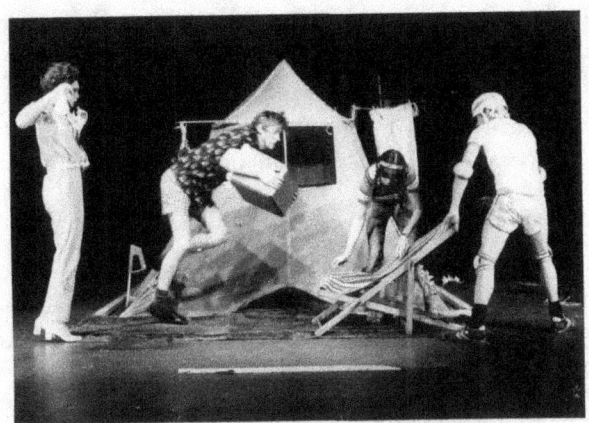

The Go Anywhere Show - The setting up the tent 'lahzi'.
L – R Caz Howard, Peter Finlay, Hannie Rayson, Tony Kishawi

Peter Finlay:

> The best part of *The Go Anywhere Show* was the tent setting up routine. Tony was like a Bart Simpson. Hannie was the goody daughter. It was really like *The Simpsons*. Susie Fraser played the pompous sister-in-law. I came up with the Dickens family and their [unemployed] situation. Hannie came up with the dialogue. We performed it all over the Eastern Suburbs over a number of months including shopping centres, Uni cafeterias, Outside town halls. And In classrooms.

Susie Fraser:

> *The Go Anywhere Show* - that was first thing we made with Robin Laurie and was very much designed to be our calling card…We did it in shopping centres. Ghastly big shopping centres like Forest Gate. We did it in the Lygon Street Festa. We put the tent up as a square dance and whole notion was that it was a portable show. Pete Finlay's character was supposedly looking for gold with a metal detector. We were an unemployed middle class family but we told everyone we were just on holiday – there was a lot of unemployment at the time. We group devised it with Robin (Laurie) It was Commedia della'arte based But we did look at that desire to keep up being a winner when you were actually desperate. It was about keeping up appearances. Caz was mum, and dad was Pete Finlay and Tony and Hannie were the brother and sister I was the aunt.

The tent, with its flimsy impermanence, its portability and affordability, was an ideal theatrical platform for a travelling 'location' show e. In fact tents would occupy a central place within three TheatreWorks shows including the revival of the *Go Anywhere Show* as the *Dick And Dolly Dickens Show* produced by TheatreWorks Troupe in 1984 (see below) and the camping holiday disaster story *On Shifting Sandshoes* (Paul Davies 1988).

Another recurring trope in the TheatreWorks canon relates to transport (public and private). Born in part out of a sense of the remoteness of Melbourne's vast eastern suburbs, the first expression of this was Peter Finlay's play about car culture.

JULY 23 – AUGUST 8, 1981

THE MIDDLE OF THE ROAD SHOW

Location: Phoenix Theatre, Burwood State College
Script: Peter Finlay
Director Peter Finlay
Design: Peter Sommerfeld, Tony Kishawi
Cast: Caz Howard (Diana Crayford), Peter Finlay, Hannie Rayson, Tony Kishawi (Doug Perrier), Susie Fraser, Peter Sommerfeld (Sir Max Faber), The Phoenix Players: Merle Forrest, Richard Fly, Brett Stewart, Leanne Thorpe, Lyn Saunders, Jo Ham, Jo Boundy, John Fenelon, Colin Browne.

The Middle of The Road Show
L-R Caz Howard, Peter Sommerfeld, Brett Steward, (unknown), Tony Kishawi

From the programme: "In 1948 the first Holden was launched. Twenty five years later in 1975, the world began running out of petrol. It's now 1981. How long will the petrol last?"[6]

The Middle of the Road Show was a play 'about the effect of the car on our lives. The first half takes place in 1948 in a small radio station in Melbourne. A special musical program is being presented to celebrate a great new event for Australia. The launching of the FX Holden, the first complete Australian car... The Second half takes us forward to 1981 as ten ordinary people journey on the roads of Melbourne. To a radio soundtrack of patter and pop, we experience with them the split-second dramas, the near misses, the small triumphs of a Night On the Road..." [7]

Made with the participation of the Holden designer Sir Lawrence Hartnett, CBE (managing director of GMH 1934-1947) *The Middle of The Road Show* took the culture of the motor car as its theme. Above all else, the private car made Melbourne's suburban sprawl possible in the first place. In the post world war two decades the cheap land and residential amenity offered by the region east of the Melbourne saw it occupied by a seemingly endless wave of backyards and brick veneer.

>Peter Finlay:
>
>"Hannie's play *Mary* was supposed to be next but she had trouble writing it. So it I had to do the next one. Which was really two plays. The first one was done as a radio show that dealt with the production of the first Holden. Sir Laurence Hartnett, the managing director of General Motors Holden and a key figure in producing Australia's first car had written a book and we consulted with him. So Peter Sommerfeld and I and worked with the Phoenix Players (a local theatre group) on that story which was the first half of the show – a special radio programme designed to launch the car. Then a bunch of Burwood State College students, 'the Special FX' did a movement based piece about car culture in the eastern suburbs. Again in working with the community we might come up with the ideas (to do a play about transport in the eastern suburbs) but it could go anywhere.

---

[6] TheatreWorks Archive, Newsletters & Annual Reports, Fryer Library Brisbane
[7] Middle of The Road Show programme notes.

FEBRURARY – DECEMBER 1981

INTERPLAY

Location: Bennetswood Primary School
Script: Group devised drama workshops integrating students from Bennetswood and NADRASCA (Nunawading and District Retarded and Spastic Children's Association) Primary Schools.
Cast: Children from both schools.
Facilitators: Bronwyn Barton, Connie Kramer, Helen Oysten, Caz Howard, Susie Fraser, Peter Finlay, Hannie Rayson, Paul Davies

Photo Paul Davies

Watching an *Interplay* Workshop
Bennetswood Primary School 1981
L-R Susie Fraser (kneeling), children from the two schools,
Caz Howard (overalls standing) Bronwyn Barton (sitting)

NADRASCA was a school for children with intellectual disabilities (most commonly downs syndrome). Drama Workshops integrating children from there with a class at Bennetswood Primary, two very different schools, revolved around structured play, including performing certain recognised behaviours such as going to a restaurant, cooking a meal, or staging a 'mini Moomba' procession complete with dragon.

"We were all very impressed with the sense of 'community in the group' and the level of integration between the children from Bennetswood Primary and NADRASCA. Observation of your programme has given us much to think about and has stimulated us to consider ways of developing programmes based on similar concepts." (Letter from Judith Blissland, Child Care Studies Department, Prahran College of Advanced Education 16/10/1981).

"I note with pleasure how eagerly our children greet the youngsters from NADRASCA each week on their arrival. The drama activities you provide are an effective means of integrating the children from both schools to their mutual benefit." (Letter from Graeme Wigney Principal Bennetswood Primary School. 12/10/1981)

1982

At the beginning of 1982 as TheatreWorks Newsletter # 1 breathlessly announced, the company was fighting for its continued existence. At the end of 1981 the Australia Council, through the instruments of its Theatre and Community Arts Boards, cut all funding to TheatreWorks, declaring that the company was "not financially viable"[8] . However, showing more faith, the Victorian Ministry for the Arts doubled its grant to the company from $15,000 to $32,000. In April 1982 a new state labour government was elected under premier John Cain prioritised community theatre initiatives and along with its sister companies, West, the Mill and MRPG, TheatreWorks was able to ride a wave of government support. Other small amounts came from the Nunadwading Arts Council, the Myer Foundation and Burwood College SRC. At which point success and an rapid enhancement of the company profile finally arrived in the form of a play on a tram.

The theme of transport and the performative tendency to occupy any available, containable public space, finally coalesced in the production that finally put TheatreWorks on the map, critically and financially. Almost from its first performance on the #42 line, the *Tram Show* caused a minor sensation. The limited seats available for each 'journey' to the city and back quickly filled and the season extended several times beyond the original Moomba Festival fortnight.

FEBRUARY 26 – JUNE 6

STORMING MONT ALBERT BY TRAM

"One of the most surreal events to animate Melbourne theatre" (Jack Hibberd, *The Age*. Melbourne June 1982).

Location: (#42 Mont Albert Tram)
Script: Paul Davies
Director: Mark Shirrefs

---

[8] TheatreWorks Annual Report January 1982 to June 1983. TheatreWorks Archive, Newsletters & Annual Reports, Fryer Library Brisbane

Cast: Mary Sitarenos, Caz Howard, Peter Finlay, Hannie Rayson, Peter Sommerfeld, Tony Kishawi, Paul Davies, Graham Stephen, Brett Stewart

Performances: 85

Audience: 4,250

Storming Mont Albert By Tram
The 'bomb-scare' scene, preview performance 25th Feb 1982
L – R   Peter Sommerfeld (Danny O'Rourke), audience members, Graham Stephen (Snr. Const. Warren Wilkinson), Hannie Rayson (sitting, Samantha Hart-Byrne), Tony Kishawi (sitting, Terry Meagher) Mary Sitarenos (Alice Katranski, conductress)

The play developed through improvisation with the cast and director Mark Shirrefs and was based on a short story by Paul Davies of the same name published in *The Springvale Journal* in January 1981. *Storming Mont Albert By Tram* generated a storm of media interest almost from the night of its first performance as people began to grasp the conceit involved: a play about a tram journey done on a travelling tram. It struck a cord with theatregoers and non-theatregoers alike. The original season, and each further extension of it, quickly booked out until collective exhaustion and Melbourne's encroaching winter made external performances too difficult... *The Tram Show* as it became known, was the subject of much press and television coverage, even a live radio broadcast on 3AW (predicting the current trend of broadcasting live performances globally via the internet, in 'real time'). *The Tram Show* also featured as an item in the

French documentary *Australie* screened in Cannes in 1983. It was 're-staged' six times over the next dozen years, running to over 300 performances in both Melbourne and Adelaide and travelling a combined distance that would have taken the #938 tram effectively half way round the world!

FEBRUARY – MAY 1982

WINLATON WORKSHOPS

Over several months drama workshops were conducted at Winlaton, a remand ('correctional') centre for girls 14-18 years old and located in the eastern suburbs at Nunawading. Some 90 girls attended. From the deputy principal.

> "Young people are being cut off from participating in meaningful experiences and are increasingly resorting to crime, drugs, and alcohol as a means of escape. Groups such as TheatreWorks encourage young people to participate in experiences that have meaning for them to thin for themselves, to reflect upon issues, and to react to social pressures in socially responsible ways. The contribution of drama personnel from Drama Workshops has been quite outstanding form many points of view."
> Elizabeth Amos Deputy Principal, Winlaton Centre.

MARCH - APRIL 1982

During Easter 1982 the TheatreWorks ensemble took a week off from the *Tram Show* to hold a company retreat at Edrom Lodge near Eden in New South Wales where they sought to lay out future priorities and discuss future areas of work. It was clear, in the wake of the *Tram Show* that another location play would be high on the agenda. The company was shifting from its original community-oriented starting point (according to the classic definition) and more towards alternative modes of production. Inspiration would still come from the suburban milieu, and staging opportunities looked for outside traditional theatres. The social catchment for narratives would still be the suburban heartland, but the re-enactments of same would become more exclusively professional.

The debate about professional standards and the intermingling of 'professional' and 'amateur' performers in Community Theatre productions was another fault line in the Community/Alternative debate.

The issue also became a union one. In principle TheatreWorks always sought to pay its workers Actors Equity minimums (which were often less than the going rate for professional actors anyway, especially in the screen related – film and television –field).

Apart from anything else, the more experimental plays carried a certain physical risk. Although nobody was seriously injured in *the Tram Show's* twelve year history (apart from its author – twice) Peter Finlay, Mary Sitarenos and Hannie Rayson all recall a tragic car accident they were almost part of, en route to one performance of *The Tram Show*.

> Hannie Rayson:
>> The hardest part [was] going on after seeing this traffic accident, in which a woman was virtually killed in front of us, and doing the [*Tram*] show that night with glass shards from the shattered shop front in my hair. And going back afterwards to Mary and Peter's (Finlay) flat in St. Kilda where we all slept together. We were just freaked. We had to be pretty close to do that. I knew that I was shaky and I didn't want to go home. My abiding memory was of pushing Mardi (Sommerfeld, Peter's daughter) forward to avoid being hit by the car and it was this woman just behind us, who was slammed up against shop window."[9]

This shift from 'Community' towards 'Alternative' modes of production for the company coincided with a name change to *TheatreWorks* proper, formally dropping the "Eastern Suburbs Community" tag. However, as the 82-83 annual report reiterated:

> "As a company we are committed to two kinds of theatrical endeavour: to the staging of professional, original Australian theatre, as well as the managed of other processes which teach us about the community we work within. And we feel this double thrust has paid off because it has ensured our more traditional theatrical product is fed, creatively, from the people who come to see it. The result is a special kind of relationship between performer and audience this is not available to conventional, mainstream companies... [Audiences] feel they are not merely theatrical consumers in the accepted sense, but that they have participated in an event that goes

---

[9] Hannie Rayson, Personal Interview Fitzroy 11/3/2010

beyond the mere witnessing of character, plot and scenery."

It also coincided with a geographic move closer in, away from the outer eastern suburbs to the Canterbury Gardens Centre, which offered an office, workshop and rehearsal space, but still not a proper performance venue as such. The first project mounted here was *Women of Three Generations*, focusing in on the family and personal histories of local women, both young and old, and again, bringing nominal opposites together, exploring notions of community through examining the differences as well as similarities. The calendar of events for the project through June and July included writing and story telling workshops (coordinated by Hannie Rayson) lectures and performances by visiting female artists (including talks entitled "The Decision of Mothering" and Susie Fraser's *Abortion Piece*) plus screenings of women's films, cooking, fitness and dance classes.

JUNE 7 – JULY 29, 1982

WOMEN OF THREE GENERATIONS

Location: Canterbury Gardens Centre.
Script: Group devised workshops with women from the eastern suburbs, including performance, writing, design. These were led by Susie Fraser, Caz Howard, Hannie Rayson.
Attendance: 945

Women from a couple of generations trying on
Dame Margaret Guilfoyle's hat collection.
Front Row: Caz Howard and Susie Fraser, local women
Back Row: Hannie Rayson, Shirley Sydenham (2nd Right)

From a company pitch document (circa July 1982):

> *Women of Three Generations is* designed as a "multi arts community project" based in Canterbury…[in order] to bring together women artists and women from Canterbury to explore the topic 'Women Of Three Generations' because changes in women's roles have affected the relationships between generations…[and also] to enable women to claim the things that are important to them and to look at them in a public forum…to enable the material of women's lives to be seen as relevant and valid source material for artistic endeavour. (Projected Cost: 18,905
> Funding sought 11,500)[10]

Susie Fraser:

> *Women of Three Generations* – I dreamt that one up. We were a bit earnest. There was a lot of stuff in the press at the time about our generation being the first feminist one and everything I read about the 1890s and 1920s [showed

---

[10] TheatreWorks pitch document 1982, Box 9, Fryer Library Brisbane

that those periods] had been important times for women and so it seemed arrogant to say we were the first…We went to the Baptist home for the elderly, got some fantastic women in their 80s and girls from Fintona [high school]. It was partly blue ribbon, (former premier) Dick Hamer's daughter took part in it. Also a girl from prison who had had a baby adopted out. Quite big stories, and it did feel it was part of that consciousness raising. Some women found it very formative in making them think about being a woman. But we always wanted to gather it together as a thread…"[11]

Twelve months later that thread would lead to *Herstory*.

SEPTEMBER 7 – OCTOBER 1 & DECEMBER 1982

MARY

Location: 1st season: Playbox Theatre (Upstairs)
2nd Season Universal Theatre, Fitzroy
Script: Hannie Rayson
Direction: Susie Fraser
Design: Peter Sommerfeld
Cast: Mary Sitarenos, Terza Loizou, Joy Dunstan, Joy Mitchell.
Audience: 4,885

---

[11] Susie Fraser Personal Interview, St. Kilda 15/2/2010

Mary
Joy Dunstan, Mary Sitarenos
Girlfriends cross the ethnic/suburban divide

In December 1980 Hannie Rayson received an award from the Queens Silver Jubilee Trust to research and write *Mary*. And later a special projects grant from the Australia Council of $4,000 went towards its production in 1982.

> Hannie Rayson:
>> When I began the process of researching *Mary* I was very conscious of the fact that I was a fifth generation Australian attempting to write a play about the experiences of Greek women living in Melbourne. I was concerned on one level that the Greek community itself might regard my intentions with a degree of suspicion but also whether I could in fact truthfully tap into a cultural milieu so different from my own. With

> regard to the Greek community, my fears were dispelled rapidly..." [12]

> I lived in Collingwood and I wondered where they had gone. All the united nations. The Greek community had gone East. I did everything Greek. I worked with a high school, Doncaster East. I went once a week, acclimatized to how they talked and their interests. Then I worked with a Greek youth group at Box Hill and *Mary* came from their stories all the difficulties with parents."[13]

The play as such is a study of the tensions and conflicts between new and old Australians. As far back as *The Shifting Heart* this has proved a fruitful ground for Australian playwrights. But *Mary* is also an examination of the tensions and conflicts within families – in particular between mothers and their daughters." (Leonard Radic *The Age,* Melbourne December 1982)

> " 'You're talking like an Australian – you got no respect', says the Greek mother to her daughter Mary. The audience of Australians and Greeks and Greek Australians breaks up with laughter " (Laurie Landray, *The Herald* December 1982)

Yet despite these successes and with the Tram Show and Mary taking 30,000 and 18,000 respectively the company still finished the year with a Deficit of 44951 out of a total budget of $106,240. When subtracted from accumulated funds, this left the company merely $234.95 in the black! – approximately the weekly wage of an actor receiving the 'Equity minimum' at this time, the benchmark by which TheatreWorks measured its professional status.

---

[12] Hannie Rayson, Programme Notes to *Mary* 1982 TheatreWorks Archive Box # Fryer Library Brisbane
[13] Hannie Rayson, Personal Interview Fitzroy 11/3/2010

1983

In 1983 TheatreWorks was successful in further increasing its grant from the Victorian Ministry for the Arts from $32,000 to $45,000, and additionally, and no doubt assisted by the high profile success of *The Tram Show* the company was able once again to secure $15,000 from the federal body, the Australia Council's Theatre Board. This went towards a project examining the nature of work in the Eastern Suburbs (*Couch 22*) and a production of *Herstory* based on the Women of Three Generations project.

FEBRUARY 24 – APRIL 17 1983

<u>**BREAKING UP IN BALWYN**</u> *A toast to money marriage and divorce*

Location: MV 'Yarra Princess' - sailing from Princes Bridge to Hawthorn (Herron Island) and back
Script: Paul Davies
Direction: Mark Shirrefs
Cast: Caz Howard, Peter Sommerfeld, Susie Fraser, Hannie Rayson, Peter Finlay, Mary Sitarenos, Paul Davies
Performances: 50
Audience: 3000

Breaking Up In Balwyn
Mary Sitarenos re-enters from her rubber raft
as the 'French-maid' Lurlene Fowler

Once again TheatreWorks timed its first 1983 production to coincide with Melbourne's popular Moomba festival – an event more associated with its colourful street parade and water ski-ing programme than with cultural matters. However, as a result of the success of *The Tram Show* the previous year the Moomba directors initiated a theatre extension programme which saw plays such as West's *Hard Labour Mate* and Nigel Triffet's *Secrets* (mounted by Handspan puppet theatre) produced. Along with these TheatreWorks offered the sequel to *The Tram Show*: *Breaking Up in Balwyn*. Moomba offered a guarantee against loss of $10,000 which enabled TheatreWorks to hire the MV 'Yarra Princess' as the location for the play.

promising to do for divorce what *Dimboola* had done for marriage, the *Boat Show* brought together some of the same characters first introduced in the *Tram Show* for what was essentially an 'inverted' wedding ceremony in the form of a divorce celebration. It was staged on a not uncommon venue for such, namely the party boat, 'MV Yarra Princess' motored up the Yarra River from the city to Hawthorn and back. Like the tram, characters boarded or exited the vehicle as it moved along. Although here those points of transition were much more limited (to jetties instead of tram stops).

JULY 1983
HERSTORY

Location: Maverston Hall, Camberwell
Script: Susie Fraser, Caz Howard, Hannie Rayson, Peter Sommerfeld, Paul Davies (based on the *Women Of Three Generations* workshops)
Cast: Caz Howard, Susie Fraser

Herstory
Susie Fraser and Caz Howard, back to back in the 1920s

Herstory is a classic example of the 'play back' function provided by a Community Theatre as defined by Richard Fotheringham where "the community and the artists devise a performance project with the intention, not only of entertaining, but also of saying something about the community's life experiences, memories of the past, and hopes and fears for the future"[14].

Herstory was a direct outcome of the *Women Of Three Generations* project drawing its source material directly from the stories that came out of those earlier workshops (including letters and memorials from the two performers own mothers). At certain times in the play Caz Howard and Susie Fraser introduced elements of their own stories as women of the

---

[14] *Community Theatre in Australia.* Ed. Fotheringham, Richard. North Ryde NSW: Methuen, 1987. Print. 20.

Second Generation – the baby boomers. One of the recurring themes of *Herstory* was the difficulties women experience in balancing motherhood and career.

> Susie Fraser: Caz and I were both 28. Our biological clocks were ticking and if you were going to have a child this was it. Otherwise there's the empty cradle syndrome. Women in earlier times were fed a 'populate or perish' line. But in fact women had been controlling their contraception at different times in different ways. We wanted to look at points of continuity between the generations as well as points of change." [15]

AUGUST – SEPTEMBER, OCTOBER 5 – DECEMBER 18 1983
COUCH 22

Script: Group devised workshops with the CUSH group (Camberwell Unemployed Self Help), including filmed interviews with participants and other locals.
Facilitators: Liz Honybun, Paul Davies, Peter Finlay, Mary Sitarenos.

On the Couch in Camberwell Junction
Peter Finlay, Liz Honybun

---

[15] Susie Fraser Personal Interview, St. Kilda 15/2/2010

Couch 22
CUSH actors 'occupy' busy Camberwell Junction using only a carpet and lounge chair. Paul Davies directs from behind the camera

Just as *Please Return to Sender* had enacted the 'disturb' half of TheatreWorks' agenda (of 'celebrate and disturb') by dealing with a wo/man's right to choose, so too, the *Go Anywhere Show* and the Camberwell workshops with young unemployed people, sought to highlight the fact that beneath the apparently comfortable parameters of Melbourne's leafy eastern suburbs there was a downside, namely a great deal of hidden unemployment.

> The project will specifically explore the connection of a person's identity with their status in the work force...We will also explore the nature of the word "unemployed". One can be "employed" in many tasks and not receive any remuneration... The stigma of " being unemployed" is one which people from the middle class are much less prepared to cope with. The project will explore this "hidden" nature of unemployment in the eastern suburbs" [16]

Couch 22 sought to give local young people 'a voice' through drama and film making workshops. CUSH's self reliance emphasis sat comfortably beside TheatreWorks own determination to 'do its own thing.'

---

[16] From a submission document TW Archive Box 1

SEPTEMBER – NOVEMBER 1983
YEAR NINE ARE ANIMALS

Location: High Schools throughout Victorian
Script: Richard Tulloch
Cast: Peter Sommerfeld, Peter Finlay, Susie Fraser, Caz Howard

Year 9 Are Animals
Susie Fraser getting naughty with a toilet roll. Peter Sommerfeld standing back to camera covered in toilet paper.

A good TIE show (Theatre – in – Education) was still a viable option in the early 1980s and this tour of Richard Tulloch's play kept the ensemble in work for several months.

THE ROTHERWOOD PLAN

In the meantime the Theatre Board's "Rotherwood Plan" had been published (22/4/83) which was described in its preface as "a serious attempt to assist the positive development of theatre in Australia over the next decade". This included dance, drama, puppetry, mime and young people's theatre. The context was the 'problem' that the Board had been funding 66 general grant companies across all dramatic art forms in a time of diminishing funds. In essence it described three categories of funding: national, alternative, and special projects (by companies or individuals).It then proscribed an 'ideal' number of companies in each category which it would consider funding in each state and territory. In a draft annual report TheatreWorks wrote

> The Rotherwood plan steps into that dangerous bureaucratic mire between setting consistent priorities, policy and criteria for itself to follow and interventionist behaviour. The plan envisages nationwide cultural irrigation through which just the right number of flowers will bloom in each State and Territory. Indeed, not only the right number of flowers, but one of each – a kind of Noah's ark utopia, floating on a sea of Theatre Board goodwill in which each theatrical species will be perpetuated. Not surprisingly , complications arise in such a proposal for example in pursing the objective of a national drama company ('ideally there will be") they are forced to define this animal as a hybrid without legs. A primary funding objective is that the State and Territory drama companies together will form the equivalent of a national drama company in the belief that this is preferable to the establishment of a national touring drama company. How this is national and why it is preferable are not explained…in addition to one major State company (inevitably the Melbourne Theatre Company) there are places reserved on the Ark for three additional companies which are "innovative, alternative (to a State company) community or regional" in nature.

1984

In 1984 TheatreWorks was successful in gaining $100,000 under the Commonwealth Employment Programme to support a small troupe composed of young, formerly unemployed people, set up to work professionally as a discrete ensemble within the larger company. This group, which became known as 'The TheatreWorks Troupe', as well as mounting their own shows, effectively took on the company's community outreach work, allowing the core group – the 'artistic directorate' to move on from the original intention to provide educational and leisure activity in favour of providing more 'accessible forms of entertainment'.[17]

The TheatreWorks Troupe (1984)
L – R Leonie Hurry, Debbie Helloran, Phil Ceberano,
Helen King, Kate Kantor

This additional membership saw a considerable expansion of the company in terms of shows produced, audiences reached, and people employed.

---

[17] TheatreWorks Artistic Policy document 1981, Box 1, Fryer Library Brisbane

All twenty TheatreWorkers on the company payroll as at 30th June 1984

Figure 25 is taken on the set of *Dee Jay View* : a working cinema/theatre in which the normal proscenium arch arrangement was reversed so that the drama unfolded on the raked auditorium area cleared of seats, while the audience sat up on the stage/screen area looking down. Still theatrically homeless, TheatreWorks remained in the business of finding new places to stage their spatially adventurous plays. Thus, the cinema location for Peter Sommerfeld's *Dee Jay View* in its second incarnation, while not strictly site-specific, did carry a certain resonance for a story set in a Hollywood saturated, 1960s Australia, and used the cinema as a cinema in several scenes.

MAY - JUNE 1984
DEE JAY VIEW (2ND SEASON)

>**Location:** Universal Cinema Fitzroy.
>**Script:** Peter Sommerfeld
>**Director:** Barbara Ciszewska,
>**Cast:** Caz Howard, Jeremy Stanford, Chris Barry, Suzi Rosedale, Bernadette Ryan, Peter Sommerfeld.

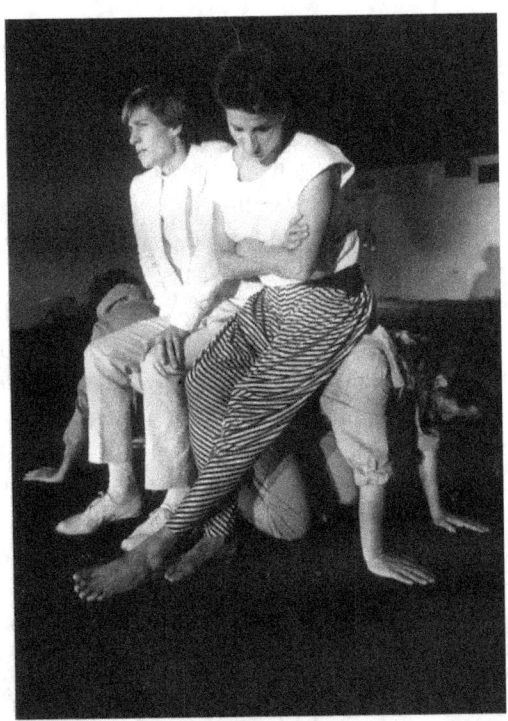

Dee Jay View
Jeremy Stanford and Suzi Rosedale occupy some human props

20 – 31 AUGUST 1984
<u>SOUTHERN AURORA</u> (VIDEO PILOT)

Script: Paul Davies
Location: Southern Aurora Interstate Express
Director: Cathy Mueller
Cast: Caz Howard, Suzie Rosedale, Peter Sommerfeld, Paul Davies, Mark Shirrefs, Susan Weiss, Peter Finlay, Mary Sitarenos.

Southern Aurora, the fourth TheatreWorks play underpinned by a theme of public/private transport, was a broad comedy set on board the iconic Melbourne- Sydney train with its classic sixties-style décor in the dining room, lounge bar and private cabins. A 15 minute video 'pilot' was produced with funding from Film Victoria for what was planned to be TheatreWorks' first feature film. However, subsequent disinterest from the funding bodies and a rejection of potential private investors by the TheatreWorks Artistic Directorate effectively saw the project shelved. Although measures were taken to redesign the story as a play staged in TheatreWorks hall using the left over set from the Bob Ellis feature *Warm*

Nights On A Slow Moving Train; which curiously enough, was also located on the 'Southern Aurora' and also involved a fair amount of surreptitious movement in and among those 'private' cabins. The TheatreWorks story was set inside the world of a failing Australian soap opera during one eventful overnight journey on the train as the production team attempt to improve their show's abysmal ratings by setting an episode in Sydney. 'Southern Aurora,' the train, took its name from the aurora borealis, an enchanting celestial light show visible in the night sky close to the south (or north) pole. The script employed the term ironically, as it dealt with the shallow concerns of television 'stars' shining nightly on a million television sets. Although never realised, any stage version of *Southern Aurora,* in a odd twist of the site-specific idea, would have involved placing the audience inside a film set, located on a stage. So the proximal potential of *The Tram Show* would have been engaged, but not the outside world going past.

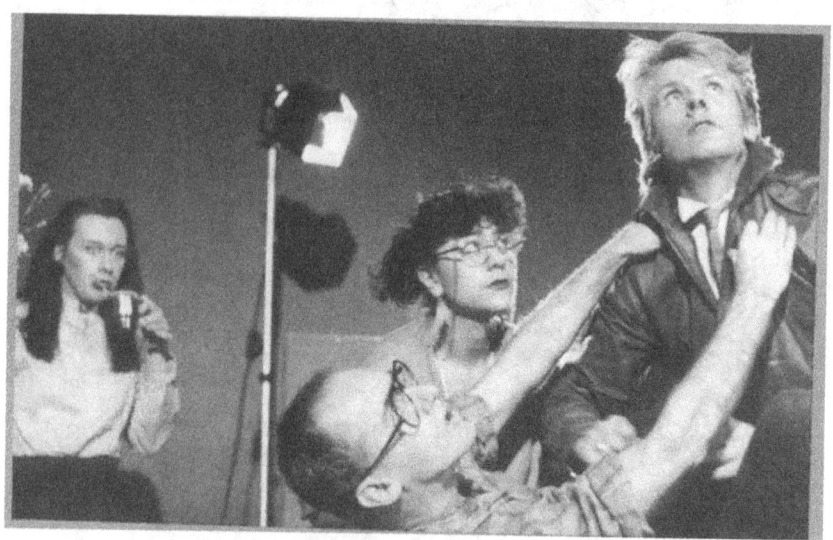

Southern Aurora
Jimmy (Peter Sommerfeld) and Nathan (Peter Finlay)
At each other's throats in the TV studio scene.
Caz Howard and Mary Sitarenos look on underwhelmed.

THROUGHOUT 1984
THE NUTRI SHOW

Location: Victorian Schools
Script: Group Devised,
Cast: TheatreWorks CEP (Commonwealth Employment Programme) troupe: John Wood-Ingram, Debbie Halloren, Leonie Hurry, Phil Ceberano, Louis Dingemans, Helen King

The Nutri Show
Debbie Halloren and Phil Ceberano,

The Nutri Show was devised by the TheatreWorks troupe to take a fairly straightforward message out to primary schools about the importance of eating healthy foods in place of sweets and other manufactured foods which generally contained too much oil, salt or sugar. When a photo of the set for *The Nutri Show* appeared in a local paper, allegedly displaying a commonly available candy bar, the Combined Confectionary Manufacturers of Australia, alerted to the main theme of the play, threatened to sue TheatreWorks for 'product defamation'. They also lobbied the Federal Arts Minister to terminate the company's funding. It was only after a humorous article by Phillip Adams appeared in the *Australian* (arguing that sugar must make people especially angry) that all action by the Confectionary Manufacturers against TheatreWorks came to a halt.

MARCH 1984
THE DICK AND DOLLY DICKENS SHOW

Locations: Camping Grounds, Schools, Shopping Centres, Street Festivals, Metropolitan and Country
Script: Group Devised
Direction: Peter Sommerfeld
Asst. Direction/Production Manager: Caz Howard
Publicist: Leonie Hurry
Choreographer: Amanda Smith
Cast: TheatreWorks CEP troupe: Phil Ceberano, (Darryl Dickens) John Wood Ingram (Dick Dickens), Kate Kantor (Daphne Dickens), Debbie Helloran (Dolly Dickens, Helen King (Desdemona Dickens),

L-R (front) Phil Ceberano, John Wood Ingram Kate Kantor, (back) Debbie Helloran, Helen King

While now more aware of the dangers of theatre with a message, but not put off by the controversy surrounding the *Nutri Show,* TheatreWorks' Troupe next reworked the *Go Anywhere Show* as *The Dick and Dolly Dickens Show* with the Troupe actors taking on the roles pioneered by the founding members.

> Leonie Hurry:
> It was very much an ongoing location piece. I was doing the bookings, the administration and tour managing, but at times I was thrown in to the cast if someone was sick or unable to perform. We did it in church halls. Mallacoota Camping ground. Caravan Parks. We did a Gippsland tour. Foster. Mallacoota. Leongatha. Came back and then did a long run down the west [Victorian] coast. We did it in camping grounds out in the open at night and in the afternoons we had a megaphone, going through the town, saying "show tonight" "come along"... "5 o'clock at the camping ground." Be there. And it would be packed. Probably it was the first time theatre had been done in those areas. I saw it as a TheatreWorks' goal to take theatre to the people rather than them come to us.[18]

SEPTEMBER 1984
JULIET AND ROMEO

Location: Victorian High Schools
Script: Roger Selleck (with apologies to W. Shakespeare)
Cast: Roger Selleck, Clare Larman

---

[18] Leonie Hurry, Personal Interview, St. Kilda 17/3/2011

Juliet and Romeo
Twisting the bard and putting the girl first
Roger Selleck, Clare Larman

1985

(photo Paul Davies)

Artistic Directorate Planning the 1985 season at the Canterbury Gardens Centre

Standing: Graeme Stephens (Publicist) Greg Marginson (Administrator)
Squatting: L-R: Peter Sommerfeld, Hannie Rayson ('Chi') Caz Howard (firmly holding the cheque book), Peter Finlay, Susie Fraser

FEBRUARY 22 - MARCH 1985
ROOM TO MOVE

Location: St. Martins Theatre South Yarra, The Playbox
Script: Hannie Rayson
Direction: Nancy Black
Cast: Caz Howard, Peter Sommerfeld, Merfyn Owen, Danny Nash, Anna McCrossen, Margaret Ricketts

Photo © Ruth Maddison

The relationship triangle at the heart of *Room To Move*
L-R Peter Sommerfeld, Caz Howard, Danny Nash

Hannie Rayson:

With *Room To Move* I needed to do something bigger [than *Mary* namely]: 'Men'. In the '70s. That defines Susie, Caz and I in that period. Caz was interested in Marxism, my conduit to being a political person was through feminism. It was big on dividing the world into what men did and what women did. Men and feminism. Theatre Works was a feminist thing. It had a feminist voice. All of us wearing overalls at the VCA. Cool overalls. Big cottontails with holes in them. We just didn't care about the effect. Hairy arms and legs. We wanted to be natural women. *Room To Move* came about because none of men I knew were male chauvinist pigs. (Laughs). They were all pretty soft. They reflected a type. I genuinely felt that women had the big emotional roles and all the men had was a few words. And I didn't feel like I knew what was happening with men. So I started having dinner with men's groups and talking to aggrieved men who've been cut out of their families. Male image, body image, how to you redefine masculinity?[19]

---

[19] Hannie Rayson, Personal Interview Fitzroy 11/3/2010

MARCH – MAY 1985
DAYS OF EMPIRE AND SLY GROG

Location: Camberwell City Hall
Script: Paul Brown (based on the History of Camberwell community workshops)
Director: Merfyn Owen
Cast: Caz Howard, TheatreWorks Troupe, Members of the Camberwell Community. In all a cast of 35 people.

Assembled cast of *Days Of Empire and Sly Grog*
On stage in the Camberwell Civic Hall

Days Of Empire and Sly Grog
Caz Howard leading a workshop with her section of the cast

Paul Brown (playwright):

> The workshop group brought quite a cynical approach to Camberwell history, attitudes which came through in parts of the play. This, and the large size of the group, suggests that Camberwell, conservative as it is, does have people interested in 'disturbing' as well as 'celebrating.' The performance was also significantly shaped by the attitudes of the people we interviewed and those which we anticipated would make up our audience. Judging from some responses to the play a problem appeared during performance in the form of understatement. Looking back, I guess we could have harnessed more powerfully the criticisms we encountered, but there was a real risk of alienating the audience and even of betraying the goodwill of community members. In Community theatre, an in particular in local history work, this dilemma is faced all the time. In this show our solution was to try to represent or please as many people as possible. I believe we were successful.

NOVEMBER 13 – DECEMBER 22 1985
THE PUB SHOW

Location: The Esplanade Hotel, St. Kilda
Script: Peter Sommerfeld
Direction: David Swann
Design: Peter Sommerfeld, Peter Aland
Cast: Caz Howard, Paul Davies, Danny Nash, Boris Connelly, Jeremy Stanford, Taya Stratton, Leonie Hurry

Photo © Ruth Maddison ?

The Pub Show
'Eat The Rich play the Gershwin Room live!
L – R Caz Howard, Jeremy Stanford, Danny Nash

Leonie Hurry:

Underlying it was the idea of sending up these rock and roll bands that suddenly went to America and became huge. Colin Hay [from *Men At Work*] came one night and he loved it. Marina Prior, Suzanne Dowling came. Thought it was great. It was hard to know what was theatre and what was real. I was sent on a mission to look for the venue. Went to the Ritz. All these venues in St. Kilda and then finally the owner of Espy offered us the sticky carpeted front room. But I said we wanted to do a live pub act. The story of a band. He said we've got this room out the back we just use for private functions. And I had a look it was perfect. 'The Gershwin Room.' Secluded. A lane next to it. Backed onto an old dressing room. It had a stage but was just used for the occasional weddings etc. It was pretty grim. It was dirty and dank. Just perfect. It's since been used as the venue for a number of television shows including *Hessie's Shed* and *Rock Wiz*[20]

LEAVING THE EAST...

Staging a play in an iconic St. Kilda landmark was not just a continuation of TheatreWorks' on going exploration of real sites in which to produce theatre, it was also designed to announce their arrival in St. Kilda and pave the way for the company to move officially from its last eastern suburban location to Melbourne's inner bay side. This represented a considerable demographic shift as there can be few more significant moves for a Community Theatre company than to change its community. In fact, the transitions from Burwood (outer suburban lower middle class) to Canterbury (inner suburban, upper middle class) to St. Kilda (inner urban grunge), can be read in retrospect as the outcome of a certain a collective unease inside the company with the communities they had chosen to base themselves in and therefore to creatively represent. To 'celebrate and disturb' was one thing, to totally identify with upper middle class values was quite another. So the question arose as to which community should TheatreWorks be doing this for ? As discussed in the chapter on *the Boat Show* (a not so successful parody of the upper middle class lifestyle), certain artistic 'crises' in the company fed a growing dissatisfaction with the choices being made. Something that was perhaps immanent from the very beginning. The company went East not so much because its founding members identified with the interests and aspirations of affluent people living in those particular suburbs, but because it was theatrically unoccupied territory – given that WEST had gone West, the Mill South, and the Murray River Performing Group, north.

Susie Fraser

So (in 1980) we were doing Hannie's *Please Return to Sender* and *DJ View* out in the Eastern Suburbs and we were already identified as a clique within the VCA. There had been West and Murray River

---

[20] Leonie Hurry, Personal Interview, St. Kilda 17/3/2011

Performing Group come out of the VCA, and Peter Oysten said he wanted a company to come out every year. We felt a bit weird going out into the Eastern Suburbs. It was a long way away.[21]

Hannie Rayson:
The Eastern suburbs in 1980. Was it a big mistake? (Laughs) I lived in Collingwood and didn't have a car, so sometimes I borrowed my boyfriend's car. It took several hours by tram. The Community of Eastern Suburbs? I felt there was no allegiance. I actively didn't like them. Because I was a tosser. The suburban experience was something I was running a million miles from. That's why I'd come to live in Fitzroy, Collingwood…Carlton. I was never going back to the suburbs. But there I was. It wasn't like WEST [theatre company]. That was something we felt keenly. They were attached to a community that they passionately wanted to represent – their values— and we didn't want to represent these values at all. So there was a sense of slight wrong-footedness. To celebrate and disturb that was the disturb part of it. Yes. That we were quite arrogantly in some ways saying that we were going to be a dissident voice. Celebrate because …in terms of the Community Theatre model we wanted to do less of the affirming and more of the challenging.[22]

Mary Sitarenos:
When we went out there it was a bit of a desert.[23]

Peter Finlay:
I used to call it Kafka country.[24]

Amanda Smith:
Caz and Susie Fraser went round to Mailing Road to get lunch, no doubt wearing their usual overalls and t-shirts and a woman from the Canterbury Gardens Centre Committee spotted them. At first she didn't recognise them because she thought they looked like 'unemployed people'. (Laughs).[25]

---

[21] Susie Fraser Personal Interview, St. Kilda 15/2/2010
[22] Hannie Rayson, Personal Interview Fitzroy 11/3/2010
[23] Mary Sitarenos, Personal Interview, Clifton Hill, 3/3/2010
[24] Peter Finlay, Personal Interview, Elwood. 12/7/2010
[25] Amanda Smith, Personal Interview ABC Radio Studios, 5/3/2010

1986

After six years of wandering the 'wilderness' of the eastern suburbs on slow trams and smelly boats, performing in community halls, schools and traditional theatres, the children of TheatreWorks finally found their promised land in the Parish Hall attached to Christ Church in Acland Street, St. Kilda. Although the magnificent sandstone Church itself was one of Victoria's oldest buildings, the Parish Hall next door was built in 1914 but never quite finished owing to a shortage of labour during the First World War. Only an (appropriately) imitation proscenium arch decorated what should have been the stage end of the Hall. To turn it into an operating theatre its high windows had to be blacked out and some rudimentary seating and rostra provided. Heating, acoustics and acquisition of a working lighting rig would also remain problems. But it was home. At last.

Photo © Ruth Maddison
Oh what a feeling...
TheatreWorks Artistic Directorate arrive in the Parish Hall, 1986
L-R Paul Davies, Caz Howard, Peter Aland,
Peter Sommerfeld, Wolfgang Wittwer (Administrator)

While the Parish Hall was being made ready, TheatreWorks staged its next location theatre piece at 'Linden', an historic mansion just down the road from the Hall and only recently purchased by St. Kilda Council for a local art gallery. While Linden itself was being renovated and restored to its former glory as one of Melbourne's outstanding late Victorian mansions, the company seized the opportunity to stage *Living Rooms* there.

JULY 17 – SEPTEMBER 1986
LIVING ROOMS

Location: 'Linden' 26 Acland St. St. Kilda
Script: Paul Davies
Direction: Caz Howard, Peter Sommerfeld, Paul Davies, Andrea Lemon
Design: Peter Aland
Cast: Caz Howard, Peter Sommerfeld, Paul Davies, Cliff Ellen, Rosie Tonkin, Kevin Cotter, Leonie Hurry
Performances: 54

Photo © Ruth Maddison
Living Rooms (1988)
Caz Howard (Monika) has angry words with her husband (Leon, off camera) in the Hallway, flanked by audience members.

Photo © Ruth Maddison

Living Rooms (1900).
Kevin Cotter and Cliff Ellen in the Drawing Room scene.
Audience watching from the sides.

From Cliff Ellen's Journal, 'Rehearsal Notes for *Living Rooms*' (obviously a work of fiction on Cliff's part):

> After the torture to the ears and body of the Chairman Mao exercises , Paul comes up with an interesting directorial point. We listen nicely. We forget...unless Caz agrees, in which case Kevin and Rosie will instantly see the light [Dark?]. Cliff asks a question, but only to stave off thoughts of an afternoon walk with Rosie. Cliff may even go so far as to discuss his costume with Little Pete, but that may be stretching credibility. Kevin suddenly discovers a hidden meaning in one of his lines and he becomes wildly excited. Caz agrees with him, but she's being nice, as in 'bullshitting'. Cliff tells Kevin he's talking crap. Try acting! No chance now as Rosie has also seen the light of Kevin's amazing insight. Leonie comes up with something from her drama teaching experiences as a parallel. She temporarily stops smiling. Paul and Little [Peter Aland] are lost but say nothing. Paul again curses his stupidity at forgetting his pad. Pete [Sommerfeld] then speaks in favour of Kevin, but it's clear he's only practicing his intellectuality. Cliff excuses himself for an instant coffee, vaguely wondering what health problems will inflict Rosie today. Cliff greets the bugs at the bottom of his cup. Probably Rosie's neck today, haven't had that one for a while.

Afternoon run through. 4PM already. Shit. Another 6pm finish. Rosie's neck playing up. Caz sympathetic. Probably caused by the emotion of Cliff telling Rosie [on the walk] that he wanted her from the very first moment he laid eyes on her -as the character- at the Gala Ball in East Melbourne. She fell for that one. What Gala bloody Ball? Mind you it may well have emanated from the bullshit she was giving me on our 'walk'. Leonie is now worried about her motivation as the Maid. Little Pete has mysteriously disappeared yet again. Must be a sale on at the Op Shop. Big Pete is having trouble with lines again. Try learning them, or is he timing it all for opening night, the old fox! Kevin is in a lather of sweat because he dropped a glass of water. He's also worried about his stupid dog. He and Rosie console one another. Paul & Caz are arguing over something. Paul will lose as he has lots to learn about women. We all pause for 10 minutes before running the second half, which gives Caz time to eat her 10th apple. Kevin finds his dog. Paul finds his pad. Leonie is smiling again. Caz thanks me for putting the effort into my walk with Rosie. No worries Caz.[26]

NOVEMBER 5 – DECEMBER 6 1986

CAKE! An Acland Street Comedy

Location: Parish Hall, Acland St. St. Kilda
Script: Bill Garner
Direction: Mark Shirrefs
Prod. Assist. Wardrobe: Peter Aland
Cast: Caz Howard, Paul Davies, Christopher Barry, Lynda Gibson, Valerie Lehman, Brian Nankervis
Admission: $14.90, $10.90

---

[26] Cliff Ellen, Personal Journal (Rehearsal Notes for *Living Rooms*)

Photo © Ruth Maddison ?

Cake! The big finale to the Paul Hester song
TheatreWorks first production in its new home
L-R Christopher Barry, Caz Howard, Brian Nankervis
Valerie Lehman, Paul Davies, Lynda Gibson,

Bill Garner:
> When the inhabitants of an Acland Street actors' agency revolt against Maxi, their agent, and leave her to fend for herself in a sadistic television icy-pole commercial, she is so traumatised by the experience that she becomes completely catatonic...so they dream up a fake hypnotist show. And the audience is entranced...[27]

---

[27] Bill Garner, Authors notes from the programme for *Cake* (TheatreWorks Archive)

Laura Gibson in *Cake*

Cake! was the first play staged in the company's new permanent home at the Parish Hall, 14 Acland Street St. Kilda and the first play commissioned from a non-core member of the company. Just down the road from the Hall lay a strip of iconic European (mostly Jewish) cake shops. These shops and associated cafés constituted one of St. Kilda's many attractions, along with the beach, the foreshore, Luna Park and the Esplanade Hotel.

1987

FEBRUARY 11 – 15 MARCH 1987
POPULAR FRONT

Location: Parish Hall Acland Street
Script: Errol O'Neill
Direction: Rob Meldrum
Design: Shaun Gurton
Cast: Caz Howard, Nick Carrafa, Kevin Harrington, Evdokia Katahanas, Dina Pinozzo, John Penman, Ian Scott

Written by Brisbane playwright Errol O'Neill, *Popular Front* was the story of Fred Paterson, still the only member of the Communist Party to be elected to a parliament in Australia (for Bowen, North Queensland in 1944).

Photo © Ruth Maddison

Popular Front
L-R Evdokia Katahanas, Kevin Harrington, Caz Howard, Dina Pinozzo, John Penman, Ian Scott, and Nick Carrafa climb the tower set.

Too good to dismantle, this Tower-of-Babel-like construction remained in situ for many succeeding productions, and was pressed into use as an all purpose, giant ladder and lighting tower.

Errol O'Neill;

> Imagine an age in which the Mass Media are very powerful, but because most of them are owned and controlled by narrow sectional interests, they never fulfill their supposed function as tools of democracy. Imagine a State in which the very machinery of representative government has been permanently sabotaged. In such an age, and in such a State, to engage in free speech and to fondly cherish the hope that Parliament will be the vehicle of democracy, are nothing short of subversive acts...In Queensland today the arts...are called upon to do what the Media have failed to do and the Parliament is incapable of doing – to subject our political, economic systems to constant scrutiny, detailed analysis and criticism.[28]

Employing by now familiar TheatreWorks tactics of audience involvement, the spectators became variously, members of parliament or present as witnesses in courtroom scenes as well as being invited to dance with the cast at the beginning of the second act. The critical response to the play was surprisingly negative with it being conceived as too long and propagandistic. Although other critics appreciated the social relevance of the play.

AUGUST 6 – 30, 1987
LAST TRAIN TO ST. KILDA ? A heavy rail story

Location: Parish Hall, Acland Street
Script: Paul Davies
Direction: Dennis Moore
Design: Greg Carroll
Images: Barry Dickens
Cast: Caz Howard, Jean Kitson, Paul Davies, Roderick Williams, Helen Trip

---

[28] Errol O'Neill, Programme Notes to *Popular Front* (TheatreWorks archive)

Photo © Ruth Maddison

Last Train To St. Kilda ?
Spying on the new neighbours
Roderick Williams (Norm Drinkwater) Helen Tripp (Dorothy Drinkwater)

A black comic look at life in St. Kilda after the closure of its famous train line.

> A play about the oldest railway line in Australia but it is not a play about the past. It's a daydream about a possible future – about the transformation of a community and perhaps the erosion of the idea of 'community' itself. [29]

Again, as in several TheatreWorks plays around this time, the main theme of the play was coming to St. Kilda and finding a place that was quite different from what had been expected.

---

[29] Paul Davies, Programme Notes to *Last Train To St. Kilda?* (TheatreWorks archive)

The St. Kilda Times referred to the play's "brilliant ideas and razor sharp observations of contemporary life." Leonard Radic felt the play was "strong on humour with fast paced direction and amiable and effective performances." The Star Observer's Chris Dobney praised Caz Howard's performance as representing an "extraordinary versatility" and found the play "delightfully entertaining and hysterically funny", comparing it to the work of Dario Fo.

NOVEMBER 15 - DECEMBER 1987
WHY PEOPLE GO TO TRAFFIC ACCIDENTS

Script Peter Sommerfeld
Design Kevin Mortensen
Cast: Peter Aland. Members of St. Kilda community.

A model of the set for *Why People Go To Traffic Accidents*
Peter Sommerfeld and artist Kevin Mortensen
Internalizing an imaginary streetscape.

Despite the title, this was not a play in the TheatreWorks plays-about-public transport tradition. Also one of the few TheatreWorks productions Caz Howard did not appear in (because she was overseas) *Why People Go To Traffic Accidents* combined Performance Art with a strong emphasis on visual expression and was partially a return to the idea of using members of the community in a TheatreWorks production, again blurring the (always vexed) amateur/professional divide.

>Peter Aland:
>> *Why People Go To Traffic Accidents* was the first play written about AIDs in Australia. And had been put off for a year because of funding. There were problems with Equity because not all the actors were professionals. Many were just local St. Kilda people, prostitutes and junkies. It was a healing process for half the cast. It was partly theatre as therapy and for me it was particularly cathartic. [Peter Aland had been diagnosed with HIV infection a few years before]. I had to stand and spin for five minutes and forty five seconds every performance. I had transformations every time I did that spin. People wanted me to go thrashing about, but that's not me. I just tried to spin faster than a dervish. Trying not to cry. Getting ready for the next scene. One audience member remained focused on me with their mouth open. Several times, there would be someone who couldn't leave the theatre as if they'd been transfixed by the whole experience. Someone else cried for two weeks and then told his girlfriend he was gay. That was Peter [Sommerfeld]'s strength, touching people.[30]

Kevin Mortensen's participation was made possible through a Special Projects Grant from the Visual Arts Board of the Australia Council. The theatre was transformed into a four storey urban landscape incorporating a number of different architectural styles. This landscape was populated by a number of nameless characters simply stereotyped as Woman, Young Man, Soldier, Station Master, and Man In the Tunnel. Performed in a dreamlike way with masks and amplified speech against a continuous atmospheric sound track the narrative revolved around the character of the Young Lion, an AIDS infected homosexual, who returns to 'the City' during a time of

---

[30] Peter Aland, Personal Interview East St. Kilda 7/12/2009

national celebration to rescue his sister from a life of prostitution and drug taking. Most of the dramatic tensions derived from the Young Lion's father, an ex-soldier who refuses to acknowledge the reality of the oppression and decay around him, clinging to beliefs he had fought for during the war.

1988

The bi-centennial year was in many ways the high point of TheatreWorks first iteration. In the twelve months before Caz Howard became ill, the company enjoyed three solid hits in a row. These included a much anticipated return of the *Tram Show* on the St. Kilda line, a production of Andrew Bovell's *After Dinner* at the Parish Hall and in the Christmas pantomime tradition, Paul Davies' *On Shifting Sandshoes,* the camping holiday disaster story set on Stradbroke Island. In the tradition of TheatreWorks earlier tent shows (*Go Anywhere*, and *Dick and Dolly Dickens*) *On Shifting Sandshoes* had also been designed as a site specific piece capable of being staged in camping grounds and halls during the looming holiday season. It was however only produced in the TheatreWorks space at the Parish Hall.

FEBRUARY – APRIL 1988

STORMING ST. KILDA BY TRAM

Location: #69 St. Kilda Tram
Script: Paul Davies
Direction: Mark Shirrefs
Cast: Caz Howard, Peter Finlay, Cliff Ellen, Howard Stanley, Rosie Tonkin, Liz Sadler, Ian Scott

Launching *Storming St. Kilda By Tram*
Malvern Depot February 1988
Chair of the TheatreWorks Board and Mayor of St. Kilda,
Cr. Elaine Millar sacrifices the obligatory bottle of champagne.

Rewritten for a specially devised St. Kilda –Malvern – Toorak – City route, and also to accommodate a smaller cast and thereby larger bottom line, the *Tram Show* in its much anticipated second outing, also enjoyed full houses every night and had thereby become virtually self supporting. Although, six years after its first incarnation, interactions with the street and increasing police interventions, as well worsening traffic densities combined to make staging the play increasingly problematic and certainly resulted in it running a lot longer than its original 90 minute duration.

Carole Patullo who played the 'connie' and the 'socialite' in different productions, recalls the difficulties of site-specific performance:

> The delicate thing in a real environment where there are no boundaries is that you've got to be careful as a performer in what you do. You've got to look after the audience. You're working on the structure, the text, to get it all in. And if anything goes wrong, you're working to get it back. On stage you might worry about breaking a cup say and sending shards towards the audience. But on

the tram there was so much more to worry about. Just getting on and off could be dangerous. One night in St. Kilda a guy walked into the back driver's compartment of the tram and stole Joe's bag with everyone's wallets in it.[31]

Joe Irving-Spray was the 'stage manager' for the tram show and she travelled in the tram's rear driver's compartment from which she coordinated the entrances and exits of characters via a CB radio with the van carrying the actors. This travelled in front of the tram, dropping various actors off for their entrance onto the tram and picking them up after they had left it or been ejected.

Leonie Hurry also had her costume stolen from a car while getting her hair done for *The Pub Show*. On the final night of that production, all TheatreWorks' video equipment was stolen from the company van (but fortunately not the tapes made of the last performance earlier that evening). As an indicator of how different the new demographic of St. Kilda was, it was almost as if burglary was a form of tax one paid for living and working there.

APRIL 1988
THE KEEPERS

Location: TheatreWorks, Parish Hall
Script: Bob Maza
Production: Mainstreet Community Theatre Company, SA

"A play about land and its importance to Aborigines. It takes its title form a comment made by an old Aboriginal woman at the end of the play: "The land is alive. It moves. It breathes. We know because we are its keepers." But Maza's play is also concerned with the acceptance of blacks by the white community. "
(Leonard Radic *The Age* 26/4/1988)

---

[31] Carol Patullo, Personal Interview, Rye RSL, 24/2/2010

JUNE 28 – JULY 2

WRITER'S WEEK

Facilitators: Paul Davies, Shirley Sydenham

A week of script readings and workshops, a forum for writers directors and actors. Scripts included *The Driven* (Daniel Lillford) *And Look...Nor Know Each Other's Face* (Maurice Stanguard), *Mirror Mirror* (Helen Cahill) *The Note* (Susie Boisjoux), *Pickers Party* (Phil Mathews), *The Case of the Metaphysical Whore* (Steve Taylor Isobel Carmody).

AUGUST - SEPTEMBER 1988
AFTER DINNER

Script: Andrew Bovell
Direction: Kim Durban
Design: Amanda Johnson

Poster for *After Dinner*

After Dinner marked a significant development for TheatreWorks since it was the first play produced by the company where it had not had any significant input into its development. The Artistic Directorate was attracted to the play because of its "easily identifiable characters, portraying ordinary people in an ordinary situation.

NOVEMBER – DECEMBER 1988
ON SHIFTING SANDSHOES

Location: TheatreWorks Hall
Script: Paul Davies
Direction: Mark Shirrefs
Cast: David Swann, Jean Kitson, Bryan Nankervis, Ross Williams, Rosie Tonkin, Caz Howard (later replaced by Christine Keogh after Caz became ill)

Photo © Ruth Maddison
Cast and Crew of *On Shifting Sandshoes*
Working on the tan at Port Melbourne beach (doubling as Stradbroke Island)
L-R Paul Davies (script), Rosie Tonkin, Jean Kittson, Caz Howard, ('The Big Banana') Dave Swann, Ross Williams, Brian Nankervis, Mark Shirrefs (direction)

1989

Artistic Directorate: Caz Howard, Paul Davies, Wolfgang Wittwer
Associated Artists: Nancy Black Peter Finlay Bill Garner Jenny Kemp Robert Meldrum Ian Scott Shirley Sydenham Cliff Ellen Susie Fraser Leonie Hurry Andrea Lemon Denis Moore Mark Shirrefs Rosie Tonkin.

Finally on the map
TheatreWorks Artistic Directorate 1989
L-R Paul Davies, Shirley Sydenham (Publicist)
Caz Howard, Wolfgang Wittwer (Administrator)

By the end of 1989, TheatreWorks' ninth year of operations, the company had produced its 34th original play. Statistically this was the most successful year to date. Five major productions attracted 8547 patrons across 165 performances, generating $67,177 at the box office. As well, a six further productions in the TheatreWorks space by guest companies made a total of 11 major productions for the year, ensuring an almost constant use of the theatre.

From the TheatreWorks annual report for 1989:

> We seek to dramatise stories and issues that are relevant to the local community and by this means to reveal the extraordinary qualities of everyday life. We also seek through our location theatre pieces, to take theatre to people and produce it in places where it has never been done before... Our work is characterised by innovation, humour, and a strong sense of the physical. It aims to be celebratory, disturbing and provoking.[32]

In reality, Box Office income for 1989, despite the plethora of shows, was 25% down on figures from the real high water mark of 1988 ($72,586 versus $105,642 for 1988 – out of a total annual budget of around $300,00). Thus for 1989 a small deficit of $4,718 was recorded, as against a profit of $9994 the previous year. Nothing to be alarmed about, but an indication of how close to the wind a company in TheatreWorks position sailed

JANUARY – FEBRURAY 1989
FABULOUS TALES FROM THE HORSES MOUTH

Location: Blessington St. Gardens, St. Kilda
Script: Ken Harper
Direction: Ken Harper
Costumes: Meredith Rogers
Puppets: Philip Millar
Cast: Jane Bailey, Sebastian Gunner, Robert Jackson, Rebecca Morton Daryl Pellizzer Jacqui Rutten
Performances: 35 **Attendances:** 1503

---

[32] TheatreWorks Archive Fryer Library Brisbane

Written primarily as 'contemporary fairytales' for presentation during the holiday season and for travel to schools. There were four tales told in sessions of two tales each, in various parts of the Blessington Street Gardens. Like other contemporary garden shows (particularly Glen Elston's extraordinarily enduring Botanical Gardens productions of *Wind in the Willows* and *A Midsummer Night's Dream)*, the audiences for *Fabulous Tales* moved from location to location as they followed the characters around the park.

MARCH 1989
PERFECT YAHOO

Script: Peter Finlay
Direction: Robert Meldrum
Designer: Simon Barley
Cast: Peter Finlay

An adaption of *Gulliver's Travels* the centre of the play a dialogue between a man and a horse in which the man comes to realise that human kind cannot be defended against the charge of bestiality.

APRIL 3 – MAY 1989
FULL HOUSE/NO VACANCIES

Location: 'Linden', Acland Street
Script: Paul Davies
Direction: Robin Laurie
Design: Pippa Green
Cast: Caz Howard, Laura Latuada, Merfyn Owen, Brian Nankervis, Roger Selleck, Valentina Levkowicz, Phil Sumner
Performances: 42
Attendances: 3008

Photo © Ruth Maddison

Full House/No Vacancies
Hanging up the washing in Freddie's Room
Caz Howard (Rosie) and Laura Latuada (Liz)

Full House/No Vacancies was TheatreWorks second excursion down the road to 'Linden', where a similar staging strategy to *Living Rooms* was applied with the audience rotating through scenes played simultaneously in three large rooms. They then come together for a finale in the former Dining room out the back. It was an account of one night in the lives of residents of a typical St. Kilda boarding house of that era (which 'Linden' had previously been). The character list includes an aging prima donna, a failed stand-up comic, the boarding house manager/concierge, an itinerant Welshman, a working girl and one of her clients, plus a homeless pregnant woman...

MAY 25 – JUNE 17 1989
THE MISERY OF BEAUTY

Location: TheatreWorks
Script: Wendy Joseph (adapted from Louis Nowra's novel of the same name)
Direction: Wendy Joseph
Design: Paul Newcombe Jacqui Everett, Robert Gebert
Music: Sam Mallet
Cast: Glenn Hunt, Robert Lyon, Kenneth MacLeod, Annie O'Shannesssy, Stephen Parratt, Carole Patullo Alex Pinder, Louise Siverson

JUNE 23 – JULY 15 1989
JACK'S DAUGHTERS

Location: TheatreWorks
Script: Patricia Cornelius
Dramaturge: Andrew Bovell
Direction: Lisa Dombroski
Cast: Joy Dunstan, Eugenia Fragos, Lynne McGranger
Music: Irene Vela

A man has been murdered. A father of three, returned solider and POW, slain. His eldest daughter admits to the crime, then his middle daughter confesses that she and she alone is the murderer, that same evening the youngest daughter proclaims her guilt. *Jack's Daughters* examines the effect of World War 11 on generation of men and the effect of that legacy on their children. Produced by Free Association Theatre.

AUGUST 1989
HAIRPIN BENDS

Location: Theatre Works
Script: Susie Fraser, Caz Howard, Peter Sommerfeld, Paul Davies
Cast: Caz Howard Susie Fraser
Performances: 26
Attendances: 1344

Photo © Ruth Maddison
Hairpin Bends
Caz Howard delving into the past

NOVEMBER 1989
<u>*PERFECTING MY NATURE STRIP*</u>

Script: Bill Garner and Susan Gore
Direction: Greg Carroll
Design: Greg Carroll
Performances: 24
Attendances: 1303

Perfecting My NatureStrip
Bill Garner (writer/actor) Cliff Ellen

A play about the clash of cultures taking place in the current gentrification of St. Kilda as a wealthier, younger, professional class (partially) displaced the older working class originals.

NOVEMBER 1989
A WHITE SPORTS COAT

                    Script: Tess Lyssiotis
                    Direction: Robert Draffyn
                    Designer: Simon Barley
                    Cast: Mary Sitarenos
                    Performances: 18
                    Attendances: 957

Perfecting My NatureStrip and *A White Sportscoat* were produced as a double bill of two short plays.

1990

Celebrating the first 10 years of TheatreWorks - St. Kilda Yacht Club 1990
L-R Mayor Elaine Mille (chair), Rev Phillip Hutchinson (Vicar of Christ Church), Hon. Clyde Holding MHR for Melbourne Ports, Susie Fraser, Mark Shirrefs (Artistic Directors)

By now Caz Howard had taken some long term sick leave from the company leaving Susie Fraser and Mark Shirrefs to manage the Artistic Direction of TheatreWorks in concert with the already established Associated Artists group.

APRIL 4 - APRIL 28 1990
NOT WAVING

Location: St. Kilda Junction Footy Club dressing rooms
Script: Catherine Hayes and Mary Keneally
Direction: Lois Ellis
Design: Diana Steward
Cast: Evelyn Krape, Joseph Spano, Taya Stratton

Not Waving
Evelyn Krape prepares for a stand-up performance

Not Waving was another attempt at the site-specific idea using the St. Kilda football club dressing rooms as the location for a down market comedy show.

MAY 26 – JUNE 2 1990
IN CAHOOTS

In this play the Adelaide-based Red Shed Company challenge the rituals of the Brownie Movement setting the play in a typical scout hall.

> **Location:** TheatreWorks Hall – doubling as a scout hall.
> **Script:** Melissa Reeves
> **Direction:** David Carlin
> **Design:** Tim Maddock
> **Cast:** Ullie Birve, Eileen Darley, Sally Hildyard, Tina Kald, Joey Kennedy, Alice McHenry, Gina Zoia

In *In Cahoots,* in another twist on the site-specific intention, the TheatreWorks Hall doubles as the entirely probable site for a scout meeting.

JUNE 16 – JULY 14 1990
GRASS

Script: Kevin Nemeth
Cast: Steve Scully, Peter Hosking

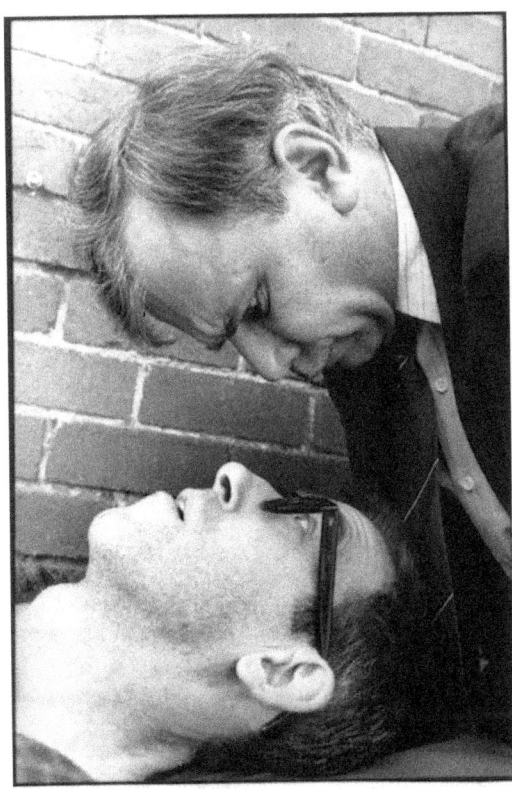

Photo © Ruth Maddison

Grass
The long eye of the law
Steve Scully   Peter Hosking

A black comedy set in the nether world of the marijuana industry near a semi-mythical town called Mt. Misery.

OCTOBER 8 – NOVEMBER 3, 1990

MAX

Location: TheatreWorks
Script: Patricia Cornelius
Direction: Susie Dee
Design: Greg Carroll
Cast: Ian Scott Jackie Kelleher

Max
Ian Scott on the poster

Max is 30 and intellectually handicapped. Max and his mother left their home when the rest of the family wanted Max institutionalised. Now they live in an inner city boarding house and earn their living selling newspapers on a city street corner. A poignant and heart warming account of the relationship between a mother and her dependent adult son. [33]

NOVEMBER 12 – DECEMBER 1, 1990
HAPPINESS

Happiness transferred to TheatreWorks from its successful season at La Mama, thus beginning a tradition of giving certain La Mama productions a show case south of the Yarra. "A play about shared households, strained friendships, doomed relationships, life, art, the universe and whose turn it is to clean up the bathroom.

Location: TheatreWorks
Script: Chris Corbet
Direction: Chris Corbet
Design: Peter Long
Cast: Melanie Beddie, Katerina Kotsonis, Anna Michael, Simon Woodward

---

[33] Patricia Cornelius *Max* Programme Notes TheatreWorks Archive.

1991

APRIL 1991
I DON'T GET PAID ENOUGH TO FIND DEAD BODIES

Location: TheatreWorks Parish Hall
Script: Laura Latuada, Kate Gillick
Cast: Laura Latuada, Kate Gillick
Direction: Susan Bamford
Music: Irene Vela

A black comedy set in the 'isolated and undervalued' world of home helpers.

APRIL 1991
BOMBONIERE

Location: TheatreWorks Parish Hall
Script: Vicki Reynolds, Anna Butera
Direction: Patricia Cornelius
Cast: Anna Butera

From 1991 to 1993, under the artistic direction of Robert Draffyn TheatreWorks achieved its second iteration. Something of the spirit of the first version of the company (with its dedication to 'location theatre') lived on, however, in the productions of the *Really Moving Theatre Company* which was registered as a business name on 17/1/1992 specifically to continue putting on the *Tram Show* as a self funded project in Melbourne, as well as taking it to Adelaide for the Fringe Festivals in 1992 and 1994.

FEBRUARY 1 – 17 APRIL
STORMING ST. KILDA BY TRAM
(Fifth Iteration of *The Tram Show* - last by TheatreWorks

Figure 48.
Audiences at half time get their group shot

Production: TheatreWorks
Location: St. Kilda – Melbourne City Tram
Script: Paul Davies
Direction: Mark Shirrefs
Cast: Sioban Tuke, Cliff Ellen, Carole Patullo, Taya Strattan, Jon Concannon, Louis Dingemans, Roger Selleck, Sally Anne Upton
Admission: $28/$18

1992

Productions of the
REALLY MOVING THEATRE COMPANY:

FEBRUARY 22 – MARCH 21 1992
STORMING GLENELG BY TRAM

Location: Glenelg – Adelaide City Tram
Production: Really Moving Theatre Company
Script: Paul Davies
Direction: Cliff Ellen
Cast: Sioban Tuke (Alice Katranski), Louis Dingemans (Terry O'Rourke) Carole Patullo (Samantha Hart-Byrne) Mark Cutler (Morris Stanley) Valentina Levkowicz (Daniella O'Rourke) Bryan Nankervis (Nigel Davidson) Suzi Rosedale (Const. Wendy Rhodes)

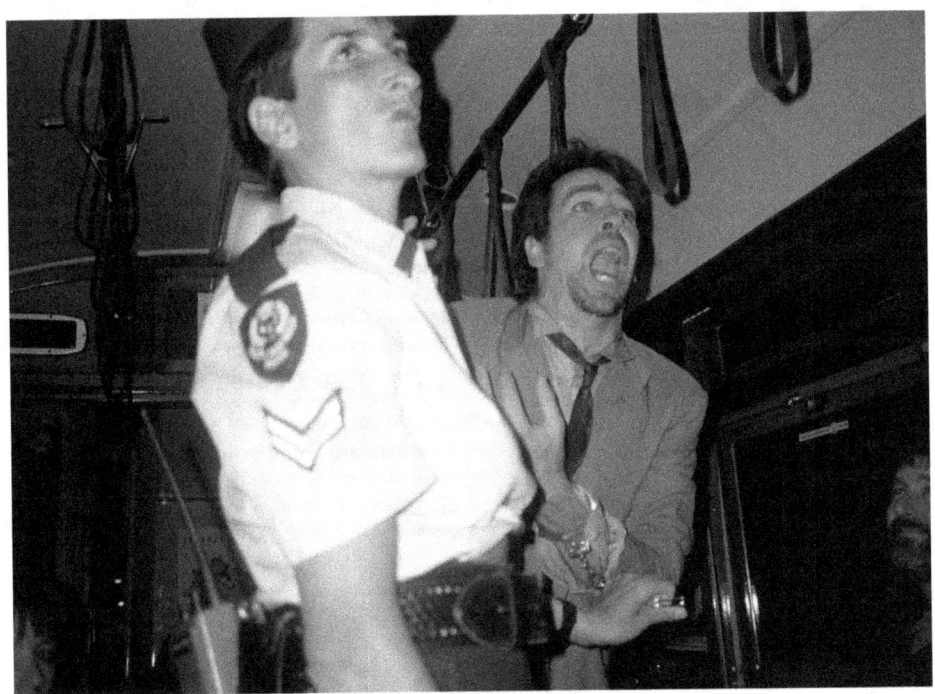

Const. Wendy Rhodes (Suzi Rosedale) arrests Nigel (Bryan Nankervis)

APRIL 1 - MAY 3 1992
STORMING MELBOURNE'S 150TH BY TRAM

Front of House (and Book Designer) Tabitha Davies front of tram

Location: St. Kilda – Melbourne City Tram
Script: Paul Davies
Direction: Cliff Ellen
Cast: Sioban Tuke (Alice Katranski), Louis Dingemans (Terry O'Rourke) Carole Patullo (Samantha Hart-Byrne) Mark Cutler (Morris Stanley) Valentina Levkowicz (Daniella O'Rourke) Brian Nankervis (Nigel Davidson) Suzi Rosedale (Const. Wendy Rhodes)
Production: Really Moving Theatre Company

OCTOBER 28 – NOVEMBER 1992
STORMING SWANSTON WALK BY TRAM
(Sixth Iteration of the Tram Show)

Location: St. Kilda – Melbourne City Tram
Script: Paul Davies
Direction: Cliff Ellen
Production: Really Moving Theatre Company
Cast: Cliff Ellen (Danny O'Rourke), Mark Cutler (Morris Stanley) Brian Nankervis (Nigel Davidson) Kay Keighery (Samantha Hart-Byrne), Carole Patullo Stephen Scully (Terry Meagher), Sioban Tuke (Alice Katranski), Andrea Swift (Const. Wendy Rhodes).

1994

FEBRUARY 20 - MARCH 20 1994
STORMING GLENELG BY TRAM
(Seventh – Final - Iteration of the *Tram Show*)

Terry (Louis Dingemans) loots the Ticket Inspector's (Mark Cutler's) money bag while he's distracted by the Connie Alice (Siohan Tuke)

Location: Glenelg – Adelaide City Tram
Script: Paul Davies
Direction: Cliff Ellen
Cast: Mark Cutler (Morris Stanley) Mathew Green (Nigel Davidson) Kay Keighery (Samantha Hart-Byrne), Carole Patullo (Daniella O'Rourke), Stephen Scully (Terry Meagher), Sioban Tuke (Alice Katranski)
Production: The Really Moving Theatre Company
Production Manager: Jo Irving Spray

Why TheatreWorks?[34]
(Origins of a Company)

Detail of a St. Kilda mosaic by Mirka Moira, showing TheatreWorks and 'Linden' (site of *Living Rooms* 1986 and *Full House/No Vacancies* 1989).

In the last chapter of *Really Moving Drama* "How Theatre Works" I examined the theoretical assumptions underpinning the production of performative heterotopia across site-specific practice generally. Here I turn to the conditions of possibility which led to TheatreWorks becoming one of the earliest exponents of the form in Australia. This achievement pre-dates even some of the more widely recognised productions of Brith Gof and Forced Entertainment in the UK, and Necessary Angel in Canada. TheatreWorks' location plays demonstrate an evolving search for *authenticity*, not only in the content and relevance of the suburban stories they sought to tell, but also in the connection between that content and the place in which it unfolded. As such, their evolution provides a benchmark for the practice going forward: a set of guidelines with demonstrated successes and pitfalls.

---

[34] From *Really Moving Drama –Taking Theatre For A Ride*, Chapter Two, Gondwana Press 2016 : available at https://www.amazon.com.au/Really-Moving-Drama-Taking-Theatre/dp/1534866752

In fact, by the time the ensemble arrived at a successful working formula (*The Tram Show*) they had, as individuals, already been dramatically occupying public spaces for some time. These included the streets and arenas of popular protest in the 1970s, where Happenings and other forms of agit-prop street theatre took place. TheatreWorks' members were also engaged in Melbourne's independent film movement where, with the aid of more portable cameras (and necessity dictated by low, or no budgets), dramatic stories were shot entirely 'on location', obviating the need for expensive sets, and again reaching for authenticity of place within the film frame. But the most significant influence pushing the company out into the found sites of its location plays was TheatreWorks' declared intention – as a community theatre company – to create and perform drama in its adopted suburban heartland and to make such work valid and relevant to that demographic. But the question "why TheatreWorks?" begs a larger question: why Melbourne?

The alleged 'Paris of the southern hemisphere',[35] with its inclement weather (desert-hot summers and Antarctic winters) has long been regarded as Australia's cultural and theatrical capital. It is also known for its large, alfresco, carnivalesque events: the Melbourne Cup, the AFL grand final with its street parade, the Moomba parade, the Grand Prix, the Tennis Open, *etc.* Here large groups of people have shown a penchant for dressing up in exaggerated, colourful costumes, happy to 'perform' their various allegiances promenade-style, inside a large massed, display.

And while all Australian cities have produced notable playwrights, Melbourne seems to have been blessed with more than its fair share from Louis Esson and Hal Porter through to Ray Lawler (First Wave), Jack Hibberd, John Romeril, Louis Nowra and David Williamson (Second Wave), and later Hannie Rayson, Daniel Keene, Barry Dickins, Andrew Bovell, Joanna Murray Smith, Patricia Cornelius, Bill Garner and others (Third or Next Wave), to name but a few, have all called Melbourne home. With Crawford Productions and the birth of Australian television drama in the 1960s thrown into the mix on top of the renaissance of Australian cinema in the 1970s, Melbourne had been a key base for the production of all forms of broadcast drama since radio allowed major producers like Crawfords to flourish in the 1940s.

The culture out of which TheatreWorks emerged therefore, was already quite dramatically literate, and thanks to a national voice awakened by the New Wave (The Pram Factory and La Mama), Melbourne audiences were receptive and open to innovative forms and new theatrical styles. By the early 1980s the focus had shifted, with the arrival of the community theatre movement, to mounting productions in

---

[35] Beunos Aires, home of the Teatro Colon above (Figure 1.1) might also compete for this title.

places where theatre had never been before: the outer suburbs and country regions occupied by Victoria's five main community companies.[36] Richard Fotheringham claims that by the mid-1980s "it was clear...community theatres...had made a profound impact nationally and internationally" (23). He goes on to list twenty-six companies who had "helped transform Australian theatre in the 1980s (24-25). In a similar vein, Geoffrey Milne argues that the mid to late 1980s, with the Church, Anthill, TheatreWorks and Playbox in full swing was "the golden age of Melbourne alternative theatre" (295).

(i) 1960s agit-prop street theatre: occupying 'public' spaces

In the wake of *les événements de Mai 1968* occupations of public and private space for iconic, political purposes – political demonstrations – often carried along with them mobile performances on the fringes. Ad hoc groups of actors, puppeteers and other activists performed in the manner of the strolling players of the Middle Ages, adopting often larger than life characters in order to caricature events and power relations or to reinforce the larger political point of the accompanying demonstration. These informal presentations were often mobile, usually transgressive, and sometimes coalesced around certain prepared (matrixed) characters. They also invited complicity from fellow demonstrators or members of the public watching on from the sidelines, as we saw in the previous chapter in relation to the *Sir Don* event. In other words, some of the key building blocks of site-specific performance were being put in place.

An overview of American protest theatre in the 1960s is provided in Dwight Steward's contemporaneous account, *Stage Left* (1968) with chapters on 'Street Theatre', 'Happenings', 'Guerrilla Theater', and 'Agit-Prop'. While Steward's book is more of a how-to-do-it manual for would-be practitioners than a scholarly critique, what characterises "Guerrilla Theater" for him is its purpose. "Guerrilla theater– like guerrilla warfare – has as its main end the disruption of an enemy's activities." But what separates it from "strong-arm takeover tactics" is that it is "entertaining" (40). Steward's suggestions for creating an item of guerrilla street theatre include having an "elastic beginning" so that a crowd has time to gather. He also urges a "definite, clearly unmistakable end" to the performance, something that GST's production of 'Sir Don' obviously lacked – as noted.

Significantly for this study, Steward also touches on ideas of authenticity and outreach that would be familiar to TheatreWorks and their 1980s audiences. He acknowledges that street theatre "doesn't call an audience together, it goes out and finds an audience in the street" (22). He also prefigures the trouble plays like *The*

---

[36] In order of appearance the companies were: The Mill, Murray River Performing Group, WEST, TheatreWorks, Crosswinds.

Tram Show would have when the authenticity of their displacement of fiction into reality (O'Toole's "Brechtian ambush" [181]) became too convincing – or confusing.

> The action of the play should represent something familiar and natural, something that is realistic, that people on the street and in houses overlooking it can relate to. But care must be exercised. Don't be overly realistic. One actor playing the part of a cop was so realistic that he was nearly mobbed by the crowd who had stopped to watch. It is necessary to inject some stylization to give the audience a degree of aesthetic distance. (*Stage Left* 22)

While such 'aesthetic distance' might tend to play against any authenticating intention, Happenings also often lacked any real story content. But importantly, what political street theatre did offer was a demonstration of the potential to take performance out into real places, away from dedicated buildings and studios. Steward concludes that "Happenings survived for two reasons: they offered variety in the means of performance (sounds, actions) and variety in *location*" (30; emphasis added).

Baz Kershaw takes this further in finding that British alternative and community theatre is

> especially interesting for the ways in which it often ignored the traditional critical categories, and made massive innovative efforts to mix celebration and social criticism, to combine carnival and satire. Here, most of the movement was engaged in the typical counter-cultural thrust of celebratory protest, and as a result it sometimes managed to create new kinds of carnivalesque agit-prop. (*Politics of Performance* 68)

In outlining the sources of "a new dramaturgy," Kershaw concludes that groups such as the San Francisco Mime troupe (like TheatreWorks) "combined Brecht and the techniques of the *commedia dell'arte* to produce popular theatre." They also drew on Artaud's theories, and in the case of The Living Theatre, they "aimed to subvert rational analysis by turning spectators into participants in excessive performative action" (*The Radical in Performance* 105).[37]

(ii) 1970s site-specific cinema: framing drama in a landscape

Authenticity of place and story, and locational flexibility in dramatic production, was also important to independent film makers of the 1970s and 1980s. New, light-weight 16mm cameras (originally developed for the newsreels of the Second World War) allowed crews to shoot virtually anywhere – especially when combined with detached

---

[37] The Popular Theatre Troupe that Richard Fotheringham formed in Brisbane with Errol O'Neill, Therese Collie and others deployed a similar mix of Brechtian and *commedia* influences to deploy often fairly direct socio-political messages.

(crystal sync) sound systems. Crews could now be smaller (cheaper) and more mobile (flexible). Throughout the 1970s Melbourne became the centre for some of the country's most important screen drama (film and television). Much of this 'industry' began with Crawford Productions and its popular police drama *Homicide*, in which the more portable film technology brought suburban locations into the crime narrative. Here Melbourne television audiences saw their own streets and back lanes become the sites of hundreds of hours (episodes) of storytelling. They heard Australian accents and a robust Australian vernacular on the small screen for the first time. In the wake of *Homicide*, place, specifically *local* places, became a popular adjunct to storytelling, to the extent that these early Australian television dramas became as popular as the imported British and American versions.[38] Local audiences connected with local stories told in local places so that the popularity of *Homicide* almost singlehandedly ushered in a golden period for Australian television production (and for Crawfords in particular).[39]

Homicide represented a considerable technical leap from Crawfords' first television drama series, the studio-based *Consider Your Verdict*. Crawfords had been the premier producer of local radio drama since its first big opportunity arrived during the 1940s when imported radio drama (on large audio disks) was effectively cut off by the disruptions of the Second World War. Thus, in addition to street protest agit-prop, a second set of influences inclining TheatreWorks members towards productions in real places was the experience they gained in the processes of independent filmmaking in Melbourne in the late 1970s.

And example of this can be seen in one of TheatreWorks' early community projects, *Couch 22* (1983) which was designed to engage with some of the (largely hidden) community of unemployed young people in Melbourne's otherwise affluent eastern suburbs. It took the form of a documentary based on interviews performed *alfresco* in places like Camberwell Junction (Figure 2.2).

---

[38] Although scrupulously based on local Melbourne killings (script editors kept a newspaper file), the broad narrative structure and style of *Homicide*, with its crime-investigation-resolution formula (police procedural) was effectively franchised from Britain's *Z Cars* and New York's *Naked City*.

[39] See Davies, Paul. "*Homicide*" *A Companion to the Australian Media*, edited by Bridget Griffin-Foley, Macquarie University (publication pending 2014). I was the last script editor on *Homicide* and the first one on Crawford's other 1970s hit series *The Sullivans*.

(photo Liz Honybun)
Figure 2.2. *Couch 22* (1983) Occupying suburban space.
Paul Davies directs CUSH members from behind the camera.

Figure 2.2 shows members of C.U.S.H. (Camberwell Unemployed Self Help) filming on location in busy Camberwell Junction. Here the TheatreWorks' cast and crew have taken 'the couch' of the title and used it to occupy a corner of public space, assuming the licence of a film crew to re-position what is usually a private space (a living room) on public land. The rug under the couch serves to further define the outer limits of this 'living room' just as the trope of the door-stop press conference carves out the performance space for *Sir Don v the Ratpack*. What took place on the couch in *Couch 22* was a series of interviews in which young people spoke of their desire to get out of their current static circumstances (up off the couch so to speak) and find work.[40]

Four years earlier, in 1979, Caz Howard, Pat Laughren and myself had produced a docu-drama about the sacking of the Whitlam government which also sought to occupy public spaces for performative purposes. As Figure 2.3 shows, certain scenes were staged in places that had themselves been overlaid by a prior (graphic) occupation in the form of graffiti. Here the text of the existing message sprayed on a wall in Collingwood ("Past, Present + Futile") is co-opted, as 'found art design', into the 'theme' of *Exits*: the sense of the powerlessness of individuals to effect (or ensure) any real political change; and the consequent debasement of democracy that follows. In essence, this is what *Exits* proposes took place on 11 Nov. 1975 – something which

---

[40] *Couch 22* Dir. Paul Davies, Liz Honybun. TheatreWorks Archive Fryer Lib.,1983. DVD.

echoes Foucault's general point about power not being held by or belonging to anybody (qtd. in Danaher, 20).

(frame capture Paul Cavell)

Figure 2.3. *Exits* 1979 Co-opting prior (graphic) occupations of public space
L-R: Paul Davies ('George'), Pat Laughren (the 'paper seller').

Curiously, it was on a tram ride home after finishing post-production on *Exits* that Caz Howard and I witnessed the events out of which the basic idea for *The Tram Show* grew.[41]

The film was a finalist in the Sydney Film Festival's Greater Union Awards in 1980, and melded documentary footage of the sacking of the Whitlam Government with fictional scenes of the personal impact on a number of people who initially meet in a cinema (the appropriately entitled 'National' Theatre, in St. Kilda). These characters proceed to engage with each other, trying to make sense of both their personal relationships and their take on the dramatic events unfolding in the larger political arena (glimpsed as spontaneous demonstrations and news items on various television sets in the background). Conceived as a "maintain your rage" project this short feature hints at political conspiracies at the top but, appropriately, can offer no firm proof of anything untoward and ends, somewhat anti-climactically, with a mysterious and

---

[41] This was an incident in the middle of Kew Juntion involving an amusing/slightly intimidating altercation, with many 'narrative' twists and turns, between an elderly drunk, a young punk and the tram's conductor, to which the police were eventually called – but only after we'd all been locked together inside the stationary tram by the conductor as he went off to seek help.

unexplained home invasion. *Exits*' broad canvas is the relation between the news media and politics and its main character is a journalist who is convinced that a coup has taken place but remains powerless to do anything about it. I summed up our intentions in *Cantrill's Filmnotes* a year later, in a way that predicts the relation between fiction and reality and the quest for authenticity that was soon to occur in TheatreWorks' location theatre experiments.

> Above all we wanted to make a film about escape and to do it in such a way that the boundaries between recorded fact and constructed fiction were always floating. In this way people might see that the emotional reaction of the characters, their assessment of the political events, is *more* valid than the dry language of the media. It followed that if Australia was still rooted in a political system devised in nineteenth century England then the whole place is still, as it then was, a kind of prison. The Whitlam years must now be seen as a failed attempt to break out of our colonial situation. That at least is the macro view. On the micro level people colonise each other. ("Exits" 19)

The personal *in* the political, and the interface between fiction and reality was a major theme in a number of John Hughes' 'speculative' documentaries that TheatreWorks members also participated in, including *Traps* (1985), *All That Is Solid* (1988), and *One Way Street: Fragments for Walter Benjamin* (1992). In *Traps,* Caz Howard plays a fictional journalist in pursuit of stories that take her on a journey to the centre of political power in Canberra. Specifically, she goes to the election tally rooms, news conferences, back rooms and editing suites of the media where she encounters and interacts with real journalists, politicians and politically committed artists. Along the way she also seeks answers to the events of 'the dismissal' after the fact: the primary focus of *Exits* five years earlier. *Traps* is described as "a provocative blend of fact and fiction, news and disinformation, conspiracy theory and the packaging of politics."[42]

---

[42] This is viewable on the Traps website at http://www.artfilms.com.au/Detail.aspx?ItemID=4132 accessed 12 Dec. 2012.

(frame capture John Hughes)

Figure 2.4. Caz Howard as 'Jude', researching the archives.

John Hughes points out that the location choices in each of his films of this period was "never accidental" (personal interview 21 Sept. 2011). In *All That Is Solid* for example, he quotes the scene set in the, again appropriately named, 'Parliament' Station (part of Melbourne's new [at that time] underground rail system). There were also scenes in *Traps* with the lone figure of the 'Jude' (Caz Howard) walking through the "incredibly alienating landscape of Canberra," signifying "someone who just doesn't know how to move around in that environment" (John Hughes personal interview 21 Sept. 2011). In the press conference scene with Prime Minister Bob Hawke following the 1984 Labour Party Conference, Hughes speaks of the "Dadaist gesture" of throwing a fictional figure ('Jude') into a demonstrably 'real' situation in order to "question its authenticity" – that is, to question the "veracity" of the press conference itself. In a revealing comment about the interplay of power relations and space, Hughes notes:

> We had Greg Heywood (now head of Fairfax) taking a macro view of the Labour Party Conference and observing how people moved around the room and who is talking to whom. We were amused by the theatrical dimension of

this way of reading the space, and how transparent these [power] relationships could be....*Traps* is a good example [of the reality/fiction interface] because the other scene that comes to mind is the use of fictional characters in an actual May Day march. We had Caz and Gwenda Wiseman (the muralist) and John Flaus ('Father Coughlin') who was playing a fictional character from another film (a second degree fictional character if you like) – come together for the march.⁴³ So the real demonstration is going on in the background and Gwenda Wiseman is an actual artist who made the banner that we see in the May Day march, thus deploying the real moment of the demo. (personal interview 21 Sept. 2011)

Hughes also refers to the design behind the symbolic occupation of the 'National Theatre' in St. Kilda as the location for the cinema scenes in *Exits* as well as 'Parliament Station' in *All That Is Solid*. However, while he questions whether scenes such as the one staged in front of the graffiti wall in *Exits* are documentary, or art-directed moments, the point to be emphasised here and the relevance of these films to TheatreWorks' spatial journey, is that there was a cross-over of personnel between filmmaking and theatre practice (Caz Howard, Peter Sommerfeld, Peter Finlay, Paul Davies, Robin Laurie, Mark Shirrefs) as well as dramatic occupations of space for liberative purposes. Hughes himself traces the tradition of occupying space for these reasons back to the productions of Melbourne's New Theatre in factories and work places in the 1930s. This story is documented in his film *The Archive Project* (2006).⁴⁴ He also refers to the work of writer, Catherine Duncan, and her adaption of the *Living Newspaper's* dramatic reportage of *Thirteen Dead* (1938), a play about a mine tragedy in Wonthaggi (which in turn became the foundational production for Melbourne's New Theatre).

---

[43] The film was *Newsfront* 1978, Dir Phil Noyce, with Bill Hunter, Gerard Kennedy, Wendy Hughes, and John Flaus. Flaus played Father Coughlan in *Newsfront* and recreated the role in *Traps*. In a subsequent comment Hughes adds:
> The idea of casting Gwenda in this way is pertinent to your thesis, as the idea here is to affirm that a form of community art was 'rescuing' the tradition of creative practice in working class movements as public art: the trade union banner, the mural. This is to affirm another kind of creative practice for the painter, just as Jude is a journalist with a community radio station, 3RRR".
> (E-mail to the author. 16 Dec. 2011)

[44] This is available at http://earlyworks.com.au/films/project/the-archive-project/. Accessed 18 Dec. 2012.

(frame capture John Hughes)

Figure 2.5. Actor Nick Lathouris holds the other side of NASA's 'blue marble' in *All That Is Solid* (John Hughes 1988)

Described by Hughes as a 'speculative documentary', *All That Is Solid,* like TheatreWorks' *On Shifting Sandshoes,* was made in the context of Australia's contested Bicentennial celebrations. Using non-narrative (or anti-narrative) techniques familiar to the music video genre, *All That Is Solid* articulates various Australian responses to the future, and takes its title from Engels and Marx's *Communist Manifesto* (45-46).[45]

John Slavin spoke of the film's

---

[45] The full quote is:
> Constant revolutionising of production, uninterrupted disturbance of all social conditions, everlasting uncertainty and agitation distinguish the bourgeois epoch from all earlier ones. All fixed, fast-frozen relations, with their train of ancient and venerable prejudices and opinions, are swept away, all new-formed ones become antiquated before they can ossify. *All that is solid* melts into air, all that is holy is profaned, and man is at last compelled to face with sober senses, his real conditions of life, and his relations with his kind. (Engels and Marx 45-46; emphasis added)

refusal to occupy any final rhetorical stance towards its subject. Within the mosaic of its various abbreviated threads, its "narratives." It suggests a pattern of rich relationships, which seem even after a second or third viewing to be inexhaustible. These implications apply to a diverse range of theses including male/female relationships, the future of the family, the effect of infancy on adulthood, the nature of sexual revenge, labor relations, the artificiality of the media, and the reification of ideas. (*The Age* "Monthly Magazine" May 1989)

Of the various connections that were forged between the New Wave theatre movement and the independent film sector (and despite the fact that both came out of the counter-cultural movement of the 1960s and 1970s), Hughes considers that such connections rely more on a synchronicity of ideas rather than an overlapping of personnel (with certain exceptions such as Robin Laurie – see Chapter Three). Another point in common was the lack of access both filmmakers and theatre workers had to any public forum for their work. Directors like Hughes who were active in the Melbourne Filmmaker's Co-operative, had little access to television networks or the cinema chains to disseminate their work. The only option was for practitioners to get together and form film cooperatives, or communally organised theatre companies. This Hughes feels was "legitimised within the ideology of the day as a counter-cultural, oppositional movement" (personal interview 21 Sept. 2011). Thus, the connection between the two expressions of narrative drama – alternative film and community theatre – was more to do with the fact that "they were making the same moves within their own traditions" (John Hughes personal interview 21 Sept. 2011). What also united them was the quest for locational authenticity. Sets implied a form of structural artificiality. The broad, common intention with both low-budget, alternative films and community theatre-making, was to *authentically* locate the action in real places.

(iii) 1980s' Community Theatre: a short history of TheatreWorks

The 'move' that members of TheatreWorks made was to set up a base at Burwood State College and incorporate themselves as the 'Eastern Suburbs Community Theatre Company Limited'. This was effected on the 23 February 1981, but right from the start the group was more colloquially known as 'TheatreWorks' and was re-incorporated as such (on 21 February 1986) after consolidating the final move into the Acland Street Parish Hall, St. Kilda (in 1985).

The foundation ensemble were all recent graduates from the Victorian College of the Arts, Drama School: Caz Howard, Peter Sommerfeld, Susie Fraser, Hannie Rayson and Peter Finlay.

(photo James Grant)

Figure 2.6 TheatreWorks founding members.
L-R: Susie Fraser, Peter Finlay, Hannie Rayson, Caz Howard, Peter Sommerfeld

From the outset the company was "committed to exploring how a group of professional actors/theatre workers can best serve the people of the Eastern Suburbs by providing an accessible form of entertainment, educational and leisure activity, through the services of a community theatre" (Artistic Policy. 1981. TheatreWorks' Archive, Fryer Lib. TS.).

A few years later these aims had evolved to include

> creating work which is pertinent to contemporary Australian lives, and which reflects the energies of urban life, building a symbolic vocabulary which will serve and sustain people in their search for meaning and identity. We aim to make our work both celebratory and disturbing. '*Celebratory*' in that a sense of wonder and curiosity is embraced and reflected in all aspects of our work. '*Disturbing*' in that we do not see our role as passively reflecting the status quo, but as intervening against certain spurious images disseminated in the mass culture, thereby opening up new channels of perception. We also seek to explore new actor/audience relationships and thereby to maximise the possibilities of the audience/participants both *identifying with the work, and evaluating* the broader issues at stake. (Artistic Policy. 1981.TheatreWorks' Archive. Fryer Lib.; emphasis added)

The 'disturb' clause hints at an already problematic relationship to the suburbs surrounding Burwood State College where the company had its first office. It also carries notions of transgression – of being, to a certain extent, and (to invoke Fiona Wilkie's phrase) "out of place" from the start. Equally important is the open-ended nature of TheatreWorks' embrace of this new audience – who would also be the chief source material for their narratives of ordinary life: stories and characters that could authentically be found inside a tram, a shopping centre, a riverboat, pub, family home or boarding house. Accessibility, complicity, mobility and connectivity would become key elements in the company's performative style, especially as TheatreWorks pursued the exploration of its self-described 'location theatre' plays.[46]

TheatreWorks was the third community theatre company to emerge from the Victorian College of the Arts. The formula of "theatre by the people, for the people, of the people,"[47] had been pioneered by WEST Theatre Company in the western suburbs of Melbourne and the Murray River Performing Group after they headed north to Albury-Wodonga (both emerging from the VCA in1979). A year before that, the Mill Theatre Company had gone south-west to Geelong and later Crosswinds (founded by Rusden graduates) would occupy the centre (of Victoria) by basing itself in the Wangaratta/Benalla district. This left TheatreWorks the demographic option of going east to Burwood.

Politically and culturally, the community theatre movement can now be read as part of a strategic plan to capitalize on the momentum building behind a wider democratization of the arts across Victoria that followed in the wake of the Cain (state) and Hawke-Keating (federal) Labour governments in the early 1980s.[48] Peter Oyston, as the inaugural Dean of Drama at the VCA, instigated the do-it-yourself and keep-it-local ethos. Oyston had returned to Melbourne from the United Kingdom at the height of the Australian 'New Wave' in 1975. Overseas he had been directing a regional repertory company, the Duke's Playhouse in Lancaster, but back in his native city, Oyston's agenda was unashamedly nationalist.

---

[46] I consciously borrowed the term 'location' from my prior experience working in independent film and mainstream television and started using it in publicity interviews and press releases to give an umbrella description of plays like *The Tram Show*. Very early pitch documents in the TheatreWorks archive, borrowing another filmic term, also talk of the *Tram Show* being a form of 'documentary theatre' implying a reality/fiction interface and a filmic (on location) intention.

[47] This was a portmanteau definition proposed by Geoffrey Milne, in a personal interview 22 Feb. 2010.

[48] Indeed in the person of Victoria's new Arts Minister, Race Mathews, there was a certain personal continuity with and restoration of a kind of Whitlamesque patronage for cultural activities across the board.

> It's important to find the Australian voice since this is who we are. Otherwise it's schizophrenic because we are a very naïve people – open and susceptible. So my attitude in starting the School of Drama at the VCA was that we would speak *our* words and I asked Sue Spunner to teach a subject called Australian History. I found a great number of students didn't know enough about the subject. And if you don't have a sense of where you come from and why you're here then how can you be responsible for expressing the dreams in theatrical terms? (personal interview 18 Feb. 2010)

It is also important to remember, as John Hughes points out, that the New Theatre had been committed to an Australian idiom as early as the 1950s. For instance, Dick Diamond's *Reedy River* (1953) was specifically a play about proclaiming an Australian cultural nationalism (email 16 Dec. 2011).

For Geoffrey Milne,
> the Second (or New) Wave was when we Australianised the Australian theatre and got the situation up to the stage where Australia became the dominant content. It was largely a mono-cultural, nationalist project. There was a fertile national imaginary that encouraged the development of an Australian culture across the board. (personal interview 11 Feb. 2010)

So if the New Theatre, and the 'New Wave' companies (the APG and Nimrod), had been about finding the Australian voice, the Community Theatre Movement was about becoming lost in the multiplicity of voices that followed (community, feminist, indigenous, multi-cultural).

But as Richard Fotheringham points out (and as TheatreWorks soon discovered), there can be many different kinds of community, based not only on geographic or socio-economic indicators, but also on criteria such as age, gender, institutional, or work situations (20). Consequently, inside the apparently amorphous suburban demographic into which TheatreWorks had launched itself, there were in fact any number of different 'communities' and the cultures associated with them. This also begs the question: what constitutes a community? As Fotheringham himself concedes, the term is difficult to define (20). One can talk about sharing something in common (a suburb, profession, religion, workplace, race, football team etc.), but I argue that one critical ingredient in the formation of 'community' is 'identity' – something that may be subjectively rather than externally or objectively driven. Hence, the search for and formation of audience subjectivities under the umbrella of an 'authentic' experience becomes the core of any community theatre ambition.

If we are to talk about the idea of creating a 'community of the audience' in the site-specific examples, this self-identification obviously involves something more than just groups of spectators viewing themselves across the sides of a thrust stage – something which Gay McAuley discusses in her recent article on Sydney theatre spaces ("Sydney Trinity" 83). With regards to *The Tram Show*, for example, the audience becomes aware of itself not only as fellow passengers sharing a journey and facing each other across an aisle, but as a separate cohort within the larger reality of the streetscape going past outside (which, as we saw, they can view through the prism of their own reflection).

The basis of the community theatre model as it emerged in Victoria in the late 1970s to early 1980s, can be readily observed in the key tenants of The Mill's artistic manifesto. The company was established in 1979 by scholar/director James McCaughey as an adjunct to the Arts Faculty at Deakin University in Geelong. McCaughey reiterates the language of Peter Brook's 'deadly theatre' when he explains that

> Part of my ideological framework was that theatre was 'dead.' It had to go into the streets and work places. If theatre is just going to be a ghetto thing, then I don't want to spend my life doing it. The mission was to explore what was the role and function of a professional theatre company in Geelong. And it sure as hell wasn't to run a repertory company. Theatre was an activity integral to all human life. I felt we had to look for ways (to enact plays) *in different locations* and societal frameworks, in which we could create the events with people, or help them create the events. (personal interview 2 Mar. 2010; emphasis added)

The ensemble that was to become TheatreWorks began to coalesce around Peter Sommerfeld and Caz Howard at the Victorian College of the Arts in 1978. In their first year there, Howard and Sommerfeld were working on projects with Susie Fraser and Peter Finlay (two actors who had been part of James McCaughey's 'Theatre Projects' ensemble). A fifth founding member, Hannie Rayson, younger than the others, came to the VCA from Melbourne University to study acting but decided to try her hand at writing – something Peter Oyston actively encouraged, giving her office space within the VCA where she wrote some of TheatreWorks' first plays (*Please Return to Sender* 1980, *The Go Anywhere Show* [with Peter Finlay]

1981 and *Mary* 1983). Later, Tony Kishawi was recruited into the core group to add his musical and busking skills: both tactically useful for the occupation of public spaces.

As Peter Finlay explains:
> I joined when the others approached me. Peter and Caz, Hannie and Susie got together first and they asked me if I wanted to join. Tony Kishawi came along later. We all got involved with *Please Return To Sender*. We liked Tony and got on well with him. But we never really regarded him as a member. He rarely did any of the heavy lifting, for funding etc. We were university educated except for Tony. Each of us was responsible for some initiative [within the setting up of the company]. But it was mainly Caz. She was a dynamo. (personal interview 12 July 2010)

Susie Fraser adds:
> Peter Finlay and I had been working with James McCaughey. We were influenced by Peter Brook: this very pared back, flexible, minimal approach where props all came off the body of the actor. We were doing our own interpretations of Greek classics...but decided we needed more training. James [McCaughey] was very 'in the head'. At the VCA we gravitated to Hannie and Caz quickly. Peter Sommerfeld, I was a little bit shy of because he was older. Pete Sommerfeld and Caz made a firm connection really early. I felt there was a sense of mutual admiration amongst us all for each other's work. (personal interview 15 Feb. 2010)

In the following decade (from 1980 to 1990) these five founding members and others who dropped in and out of the core ensemble, operated as an 'Artistic Directorate', collectively responsible for both the company's finances and its artistic direction. Membership of the 'Artistic Directorate' fluctuated over these years between principally: Caz Howard, Peter Sommerfeld, Peter Finlay, Hannie Rayson, Susie Fraser, Paul Davies, Mary Sitarenos, Merfyn Owen, Mark Shirrefs and a succession of administrators: Jill Warne, Martin Foot, Greg Marginson, Amanda Smith, and Wolfgang Wittwer. This principle of collective responsibility was in keeping with the demotic impulse that drove the company in its desire to tap into and reflect grass-roots, suburban aspirations and experience. It was also of course, a model that was applied in the collective organisation of the APG (The Pram Factory), although in TheatreWorks' case, being smaller, the democratic principle proved less unwieldy.

While not officially a member of the Artistic Directorate, designer Peter Aland nevertheless worked with the company from the early days (including on the set design of a number of site-specific plays) and he explains the decision-making process thus:

> TheatreWorks was a true democracy. It wasn't a system of taking a vote and the majority wins. It was about consensus. When there was disagreement the disagreement was looked at. Out of ten people, nine are saying let's do it this way... And one is standing out against that. The point of view of that person was taken on board...and perhaps they would finally come round. [Or maybe not]. When a personality tried to dominate they were nudged out. Compromise is the wrong word. [It was more about] 'consensus'. Coming together. But Caz and Peter [Sommerfeld], they were the spark. (personal interview 13 Nov. 2009)

One production that defined the embryonic TheatreWorks cohort while they were still students at the VCA was their production of *Fanshen* in 1978. David Hare's 1975 play about the effect of the Maoist revolution on a small village in China, with its Brechtian overtones and collective decision-making, provided a neat fit for TheatreWorks' later collaboratively-organised, community-orientated theatre practice.

Figure 2.7. *Fanshen*, 1978. The embryonic TheatreWorks' ensemble at the VCA: L-R: Susie Fraser, (Nicki Compton), Hannie Rayson, (Christof Gregory), (Amanda Ma), Peter Sommerfeld, Peter Finlay, Caz Howard.[49]

---

[49] The bracketed actors were not founding members.

Again, Susie Fraser recalls it this way:

> *Fanshen.* That was another defining moment. Some people did Tennessee Williams and we did *Fanshen* [laughs]. That set us apart. It was huge transcripts based on a lot of doco material from the Chinese revolution and it wasn't about practicing your emotive acting, it was more Brechtian and group work, and ensemble. (personal interview 15 Feb. 2010.)

Certainly it was Caz Howard, with her combination of performance and management skills,[50] along with Peter Sommerfeld and his connection to Burwood State College, who principally urged the company into being. Of the five founding members, however, Caz was the only one to stay continuously on deck in the first decade and to see TheatreWorks through its many ups and downs, until her year long battle with cancer ended, sadly, in May 1990. Caz's centrality to, and her omnipresence in, the company's catalogue of works only becomes clear with hindsight – as it is documented in the attached TheatreWorks' chronology. Her involvement in virtually all of these early productions can now be more clearly recognised with the advantage of hindsight.

Yet as Susie Fraser also points out:

> There were people [at the Victorian College of the Arts] who wanted to be MTC [Melbourne Theatre Company] performers. We never did. We must've been hard to teach. I didn't want someone to tell me what theatre to make, I wanted the skills. We already had some sense of making our own work. So we were drawn together before there was any sense of a company...We thought we were intellectual, radical idealists. We didn't think we were what most people called 'community theatre'. (personal interview 15 Feb. 2010)

Fraser's last point hints at a conflicted approach to the task that lay before the nascent site-specific company. Its work would, by definition (as a 'community' company), be inevitably tied to a particular geography (initially the outer eastern suburbs). The journey the company was to undertake from the far eastern to Melbourne's inner-urban demographic was emblematic of an evolving search for, not only new suburban stories to tell, but ever more inventive and challenging places and communities in which to tell them. I argue this was also a search for authenticity, not just in terms of the resonance of spatial and demographic relationships, but in the

---

[50] Caz had studied Economics at the University of Queensland and subsequently trained on the very early computer systems of a major bank.

particularly close bond the company wanted to forge with its intended audiences. This connection was strained in Melbourne's more affluent 'middle-eastern suburbs' (Canterbury-Camberwell) because of a disjunction between TheatreWorks' alternative ideology and the innate political conservatism of the area.

(iv) The cultures of suburbia: discovering an *authentic* community

The term 'suburban' implies something *'less* than urban', lower in the hierarchy, bland, away from the centre of things, of minor significance, often co-joined to the idea of 'wasteland'. What TheatreWorks encountered when it initially based itself at Burwood State College was something Donald Horne had identified almost a generation earlier. The comment from *The Lucky Country* included on the opening page of TheatreWorks' first pitch document to the funding bodies was Horne's assertion that

> The profusion of life doesn't wither because people live in small brick houses with red tile roofs. It is the almost universal failure of Australian writers to realise this that causes them either to caricature Australian life, or to ignore it… Almost all Australian writers, whatever their politics, are reactionaries whose attitude to the massive diversities of suburban life is to ignore it or to condemn it rather than discover what it is. (18)

This is essentially what the TheatreWorks' project set out to do: to discover who their audiences were, and to reflect that discovery back in order to create a culture of live theatre in the suburbs where there had been none. This process was intentionally strategic, and determinedly professional. As Peter Oyston admits: "I had a map [of Victoria] on the wall of my office with the various population densities, giving us an insight into where new companies could go…you must start from a sense of place" (personal interview 18 Feb. 2010). Integral to this 'sense of place' was a broad understanding of the cultural and social forces that had shaped it. To this extent, the approach needed to be authentically based, in other words: appropriate and valid for the community targeted.

Strategic mobility was also inherent in the TheatreWorks' business plan because, in its first five years of operations (until the move St. Kilda's Parish Hall in 1985), the company did not have a proper performance space of its own. Not surprisingly, in these peripatetic years, a certain restlessness characterized both the company and the content of its activities. Plays produced from 1980 to 1984 had to be flexible enough to be tour-able. Consequently, they were designed to be mounted in any available hall or class room, park or street: both internal and external spaces. Initially, therefore, the elements of mobility and accessibility to be found in the early plays were the outcome of a certain corporate homelessness. The search for new performance spaces was leading TheatreWorks increasingly out into the open, to the public spaces (including public transport) which a prior tradition of agit-prop street theatre had already occupied.

The first official TheatreWorks' production was Hannie Rayson's *Please Return To Sender* staged in their final year at the VCA (1980). The set was a scaffolding construction (Figure 2.8) designed to take the play into various eastern suburban locations, including Box Hill Community Centre, Rusden State College, the Spastic Society, Glen Waverly Centre Hall, Camberwell Civic Theatrette, Nunawading Community Centre, and the Syndal Hall. Later touring shows were considerably less unwieldy and indeed, *The Go Anywhere Show* produced the following year (1981), revolved around a much more portable tent (Chapter Three). Yet mobility is clearly present in the company's work from *Please Return to Sender* on: the idea of moving out, of taking theatre into the suburbs where it had rarely been before, at least in a 'professional' sense. As James McCaughey noted, community theatre was not "simply an extension or addendum to the amateur dramatic society movement – the repertory and 'little theatre' tradition that persists in many small towns and regions" (personal interview 2 Mar 2010).

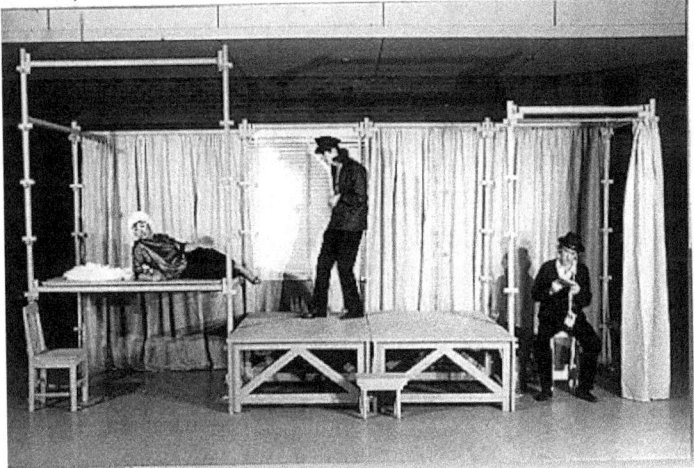

Figure 2.8. On tour with *Please Return To Sender* (Hannie Rayson 1980) The scaffolding set with rostra.[51] L–R: Susie Fraser, Peter Finlay, Peter Sommerfeld.

---

[51] Interestingly, but I'm sure completely co-incidentally, the scaffolding set, with rooms visible through each other bears a remarkable resemblance to Brith Gof's

Hannie Rayson recalls:

> We had scaffolding that framed a stage and we took that on tour around various church halls. A reverend told me, after one performance as we were washing up the cups, that "I've never enjoyed anything so much that I've disagreed with so much." What he meant was: the message in the play that abortion was an option. Stephen Lusher in 1978 had mooted in [the Victorian] parliament that abortion should be put on the agenda and members should have a conscience vote. That was the inciting incident. So I had a man get pregnant (in one testicle). It must've been at the height of my feminism [laughs]. (personal interview 11 Mar. 2010)

The overall company agenda was therefore two-fold: to situate the work in the eastern suburbs and to reflect aspects of that community back to itself, even if this involved some kind of disturbance. Although on that point Rayson, who feels she has been disturbing audiences in one way or another through her work ever since, now wonders

> to what extent we are pulling the wool over our own eyes, imaging that we were having any effect on change. We all contribute in some ways, theatre is just one way. You disturb by getting up their nose. Or you give courage, inspiration and support to your team that gives them the power to go forth and be active and militant. And that's good too. That's what theatre can do. But I don't think we made much impact on the eastern suburbs generally. (personal interview 11 Mar. 2010)

In the case of *Please Return to Sender* what theatre could do was mount a discourse about (typically for TheatreWorks) a woman's 'right to choose'. The intention to reach out into the suburban heartland and to do so in a non-hierarchical way (as an 'artistic directorate'), tends to further blur the demarcation between cultural producers and consumers. It also prepares a framework for any prospective audience to enter into the process as participants. A TheatreWorks' audience (to quote the Marxian source and inspiration for *All That Is Solid*), would be "at last compelled to face with sober senses, [their] real conditions of life, and [their] relations with [their] kind" (*Communist Manifesto* 46).

This raises the question of the content of that discourse: the stories of the suburb.

---

iconic production of McLucas's *Tri Bywyd* in a Bernard Tschumi inspired construction fifteen years later (in 1995).

The classic mechanism by which a community theatre company initiated a project was outlined by Fotheringham:

> This community approaches or is approached by, a group of professional theatre workers. Together the community and the artists devise a performance project with the intention, not only of entertaining, but also of saying something about the community's life experiences, memories of the past, and hopes and fears for the future. The theatre professionals contribute their skills in co-ordination, artistic direction, writing, design, and sometimes acting, with a major input on as many levels as possible from the amateur community participants, who may be re-enacting key moments in their lives; expressing their attitudes to life. The resulting play or theatrical event is something which other members of the same community can watch, while the subject matter encourages them to respond differently from someone watching it simply as theatre. (20)

In such a case the experience of the work may be said to be more *authentic* for those directly or indirectly involved in its creation. This process exactly describes TheatreWorks' projects such as: *Interplay, Couch 22, Days of Empire and Sly Grog, Mary, Women of Three Generations* and *Herstory*. In these examples, TheatreWorks pursued a community theatre agenda as classically defined.

For example, Hannie Rayson's second play, *Mary* (1982), deals with the Anglo-Celtic lower middle class as it finds itself suddenly sharing its suburban space with an emerging immigrant group: specifically the post-war, southern European 'New Australians' (Greeks and Italians).

Figure 2.9 *Mary* Hannie Rayson (1982)
Joy Dunstan, Mary Sitarenos.

This ethnic community had started their upwardly mobile journey from the cafes of the inner city and the manufacturing industries of the western suburbs and now saw their second and third generations set off in search of a better life in Melbourne's vast eastern suburban spread. In *Mary* there is also a clash of generational communities as the younger members of different ethnic groupings share a sub-culture related more to the interests of their own age. And it was in the conflicting claims of these various 'community' agendas (age, ethnicity, class) that the drama of *Mary* resides. Another feminist inspired 'TheatreWork', *Mary* was as much a play about what the daughters have in common as what the mothers don't.

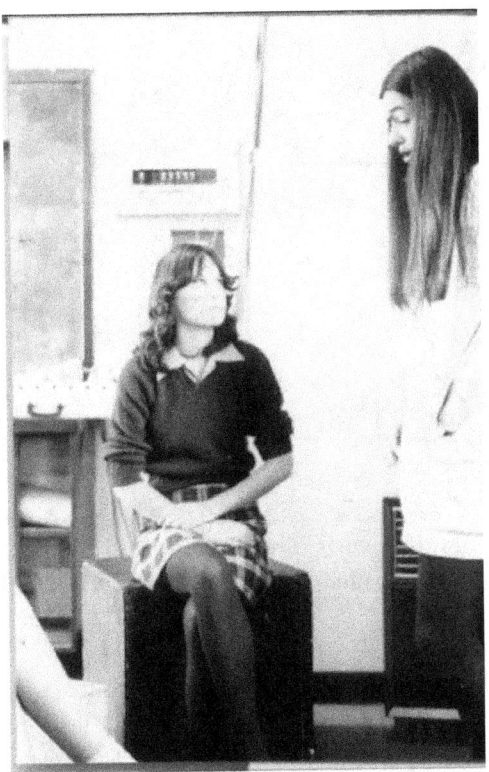

Figure 2.10 Hannie Rayson workshopping *Mary* with students from Doncaster East high school 1981

Rayson recalls that when she began the process of writing *Mary* she was very conscious of the fact that

> I was a fifth generation Australian attempting to write a play about the experiences of Greek women living in Melbourne. I was concerned on one level that the Greek community itself might regard my intentions with a degree of suspicion, but also whether I could in fact truthfully tap into a cultural milieu so different from my own. With regard to the Greek community, my fears were dispelled rapidly..." (personal interview 11 Mar. 2010)

Another community project where gender issues were paramount was *Women of Three Generations* which brought together women of all ages from across the eastern suburbs. It mainly consisted of a series of workshops that included performance, writing and filmmaking. These were designed and led by TheatreWorks' own feminist triumvirate of Susie Fraser, Caz Howard and Hannie Rayson.

Figure 2.11. *Women of Three Generations* (1982). Performance workshop modelling Dame Margaret Guilfoyle's hat collection.

Women of Three Generations was designed as a "multi-arts community project" based in Canterbury. It sought to bring together female artists and local women in order to explore the topic 'Women Of Three Generations'.

> because changes in women's roles have affected the relationships between generations...[and also] to enable women to claim the things that are important to them and to look at them in a public forum...to enable the material of women's lives to be seen as relevant and valid source material for artistic endeavour. (Company Documents. 1983. TheatreWorks Archive. Fryer Lib. TS)

Herstory, a group-devised play performed by Caz Howard and Susie Fraser, drew on the material gathered through the *Women of Three Generations* project to explore the lives of women over the twentieth century with the focus very much on the struggle for equality. Both strands of the project: the community oriented workshops and the professionally produced play, affirm Helen Gilbert and Joanne Tompkins' point about post-colonial histories:

> Re-visioning history also enables the reinstatement of interest groups who have been left out of the official records because they were victims of prejudice or punishment, or because they were denied an opportunity to speak. The recuperation of women's histories is particularly relevant here and has been a fundamental task for women all over the world. (*Post Colonial Drama* 118)

In exactly this spirit *Herstory* sought to acknowledge and thereby 'celebrate' women's achievements over three generations and a turbulent century.

(v) Forming the 'community of the audience': fashioning subjectivities

All these factors: community outreach, corporate homelessness, a background in independent filmmaking, the necessity to keep moving in street demonstrations, Melbourne's 1980s comedy revolution, consciously seeking authenticity in new actor-audience relationships, the visceral component – all coalesced to create a form of site-specific artefact that was playful, inventive and popular. These qualities also instituted the formation of the community of the audience *within* the play: the fashioning of their subjectivity as commuters on a tram, guests at a divorce party, fans of a rock band or 'ghosts' in an historical mansion. Again, the guiding principle lay in just how convincingly that subjectivity was formed, how authentically the audience took on these disparate roles and accepted the collision of fiction into reality that was taking place in front of and (frequently) all around them.

Yet of all the community theatre companies to emerge in Victoria in the 1980s, TheatreWorks was arguably the most conflicted about who its community was exactly, and what it should be doing with them. The missionary template laid down by WEST and MRPG combined with Peter Oyston's demographic strategies combined to draw TheatreWorks out into Melbourne's eastern suburbs. But a fundamental restlessness and uncertainty saw the company move its base of operations three times in five years from Melbourne's outer-eastern Burwood, to leafy middle-eastern Canterbury, and finally to the socio-cultural melting pot of inner-urban St. Kilda.

Figure 2.12. Representations of Space VI: occupying suburban space. Indicative TheatreWorks' productions and their locations 1981-1988.

Figure 2.12 shows seven TheatreWorks' plays that were sited in the three different municipalities (and effectively very different communities) in which the company positioned itself as it moved steadily west from Burwood towards the inner city.

Given that a community theatre company is essentially concerned with reflecting the local demographic back to itself, then this progression in search of audiences and stories is reflected in the quite different content and style of the various productions that came out of the three stopping points (of Burwood, Canterbury and St. Kilda). These range from the *Go Anywhere Show, Storming Mont Albert By Tram* and *Mary* (all set in the outer east), to *Herstory* and *Breaking Up In Balwyn* (in the more up-market middle east) and finally, *The Pub Show* and *Living Rooms* in the less salubrious, but more culturally literate inner-urban demographic.

Almost from the start there was a certain ambiguity about the outer eastern suburban location in which TheatreWorks had chosen to situate itself. As Hannie Rayson admits:

> The suburban experience was something I was running a million miles from. That's why I'd come to live in Fitzroy, Collingwood, Carlton. I was never going back to the suburbs. But there I was. It wasn't like WEST. That was something we felt keenly. They were

attached to a community that they passionately wanted to represent and we didn't want to represent these [eastern suburbs] values at all. So there was a sense of slight wrong-footedness from the start. (personal interview 11 Mar. 2010)

Other founding members had similar reservations. In Susie Fraser's words, "we felt a bit weird going out into the eastern suburbs. It was a long way away" (personal interview 15 Feb. 2010). Mary Sitarenos also remembers "when we went out there it was a bit of a desert" (personal interview 3 Mar. 2010). Peter Finlay confesses that he "used to call it Kafka country" (personal Interview. 12 July 2010).

This crisis of identity reached a climax at the end of 1987, a year that had seen two problematic, traditionally-staged productions produce a disappointing box office namely, *Last Train To St. Kilda* (Paul Davies) and Errol O'Neill's *Popular Front*. At a subsequent meeting requested by TheatreWorks with the Victorian Ministry for the Arts, it was decided to address the company's split focus head on. Minutes from that meeting with Wendy Hamilton (Drama officer for the Ministry) reveal that the funding body was becoming concerned about TheatreWorks' identity as a company and its overall direction (Minutes of Company Meetings. 1987. TheatreWorks Archive. Fryer Lib. TS).

The Ministry panel appointed to assess TheatreWorks' overall performance in the wake of its location plays had wondered whether it was a "community" oriented theatre company or a "general one"? While Hamilton conceded that the question of split-identity was relevant to a number of companies at the time, she warned that the overall funding situation was "grim." In response Caz Howard argued that TheatreWorks had always been in this position and that different 'community' theatre companies had different identities. Hamilton agreed that TheatreWorks had always "blurred the edges" and that indeed, community theatre companies are different precisely because their communities were (as acknowledged by Fotheringham). I argued that every year TheatreWorks did at least one or two (out of a possible three) productions which directly reflect the issues and concerns of the local community and that these works were in turn supported by the local community, not least by a generally healthy box office (Minutes of Company Meetings.1987. TheatreWorks Archive. Fryer Lib. MS).

Additionally, all of these productions were original and by definition all 'premieres' of new Australian work. Hamilton pointed out that in the current Melbourne scene (1987), Playbox had assumed the mantle of primary producer of new Australian plays. In fact, denominating one's position at that time had become so problematic that John Sumner, artistic director of the mainstage Melbourne Theatre Company, seeking to capitalise on the current fashion, declared the MTC to be Australia's "largest community theatre company."[52]

Discussion between TheatreWorks and the Arts Ministry then turned to the formation of the 'community of the audience' and the methodologies by which audiences experienced a TheatreWorks' play – most apparent in the location examples. But the relatively small audience sizes in these works made profit margins at best, slender (Minutes of Company Meetings. 1987. TheatreWorks Archive. Fryer Lib.). As a result of this meeting and the recent departure of founding member Peter Sommerfeld, it was decided to abandon the original idea of a self-governing ensemble (an 'Artistic Directorate') in favour of a group of 'Associated Artists' – effectively an artistic board – tasked to seek out new projects, provide a base of talent to draw on, and advise on the way forward.

By the end of the 1980s, TheatreWorks, through its very presence in St. Kilda as an agent of cultural production, had become part of the change it was talking about – effectively part of the gentrification of the St. Kilda community it had finally chosen to commit to. Indeed, in a rare feat of longevity for any cultural enterprise, TheatreWorks continues to support the production of new work (much of it local), from its final destination in the Christ Church Parish Hall.[53]

---

[52] This claim, first announced in *The National Times*, was quoted, somewhat ironically, by Don Mamouney in his keynote address to the Second Community Theatre Conference at the Mill Theatre in November 1984. See Papers of the 2nd National Community Theatre Conference, Mill Theatre, Geelong November 9 – 11 1984. (TheatreWorks' Archive Fryer Lib.).

[53] Christ Church is Melbourne's oldest surviving church, built barely 16 years after European settlement in the colony. Although the TheatreWorks' space (the Parish Hall) itself dates from much later in 1914. Interestingly, the labour shortage caused by the First World War left the Parish Hall unfinished and appropriately enough for a dedicated site-specific company, only the façade of the intended proscenium arch was ever built. In this case the stage behind this very concrete fourth wall was itself, literally 'imaginary'.

Finally on the map.
TheatreWorks' last 'Artistic Directorate' 1988.
L-R: Paul Davies, Shirley Sydenham, Caz Howard, Wolfgang Wittwer

By 1988 the company was officially on the map (Figure 2.13), an enduring participant in the suburban evolution it had set out to describe, celebrate and disturb. On its journey from the tree lined streets of outer suburban Burwood to the nocturnal pleasure sites of Port Phillip Bay, TheatreWorks had brought to the surface, for dramatic examination, something of the complex web of life that failed to wither under Donald Horne's red tiled roofs. The desire to connect with audiences was spun from a clearly articulated democratic impulse, a desire to find authentic connections with audiences through the production of performances in the public spaces of de Certeau's 'ordinary users'. This set the scene, literally, for the dramatic and moving exploration of location theatre that followed in the succeeding decade (1980s). This journey began, appropriately enough with a play in a tent.

Caz (Carolyn Lee) Howard (1952 – 1990)

TheatreWorks' co-founder and co-artistic director (1980 – 1989)

As "Maxi" in *Cake* (1986)

As an "actor" in *Herstory*

OTHER BOOKS BY PAUL DAVIES

Storming Mont Albert by Tram – one man's attempt to get home (1982)
https://www.amazon.com/Storming-Mont-Albert-Tram-Attempt/dp/0648599868
ISBN 9780648599869

Breaking Up In Balwyn – a toast to money, marriage and divorce (1983)
https://www.bookdepository.com/Breaking-Up-Balwyn-Paul-Michael-Davies/9781727112566
ISBN 2370000622402
9780648599807

Living Rooms – scenes in a family mansion (1986)
https://www.bookdepository.com/Living-Rooms-Paul-Michael-Davies/9780648599814
ISBN 9780648599814

Last Train To St. Kilda ? – a heavy rail story (1987)
https://www.bookdepository.com/Last-Train-St-Kilda-Paul-Michael-Davies/9780648599821
ISBN 9780648599821

On Shifting Sandshoes - an in tents experience (1988)
https://www.bookdepository.com/On-Shifting-Sandshoes-Paul-Michael-Davies/9780648599845
ISBN 9780648599845

Storming St. Kilda by Tram – another man's attempt to get home (1988)
https://www.booktopia.com.au/storming-st-kilda-by-tram-paul-michael-davies/book/9780648599876.html
ISBN 97806485998 76

Full House/No Vacancies – last night at the Linga Longa (1989)
https://www.bookdepository.com/Full-House-No-Vacancies-Paul-Michael-Davies/9780648599852
ISBN 9780648599852

Storming Glenelg by Tram – one woman's attempt to get home (1992/1994)
https://www.amazon.com.au/Storming-Glenelg-Tram-Womans-Attempt/dp/1976439108
ISBN 9781976439100

33 Postcards From Heaven Ustraylia – gateway to the Rainbow Coast (2005)
https://www.amazon.com/33-Postcards-Heaven-Mono-correspondance/dp/1533585032
ISBN 9780646436265

Really Moving Drama – taking theatre for a ride (2013)
https://www.amazon.com.au/Really-Moving-Drama-Taking-Theatre/dp/1534866752
ISBN 9781534866751

Smoke In Mirrors – screenwriters admit to make-believe (2020)
https://www.angusrobertson.com.au/books/smoke-in-mirrors-paul-davies/p/9780648599883?gclid=EAIaIQobChMI2tS5ldOm6wIVUX8rCh26AwQBEAQYBCABEgLKxfD_BwE

Paul Davies is an award winning screenwriter, editor and playwright who has worked on a number of television series from *Homicide* (1974-5), *The Box* (1975-76) and *The Sullivans* (1976-78) to *Skyways* (1979), *Rafferty's Rules* (1985), *Blue Heelers* (1997), *Pacific Drive* (1996), *Stingers* (1998-2003), *Headland* (2005) and *Something in the Air* (1999-2001). He also helped spark the site-specific performance revolution in Melbourne in the 1980s with TheatreWorks' production of his first play *Storming Mont Albert By Tram* (1982). What became known as *The Tram Show* played over a dozen years to packed trams in Melbourne and Adelaide, generating around a million dollars at the box office and trambulating a total distance that would have taken the production halfway around the world. Its success lead to an outbreak of 'location theatre' in Melbourne throughout the 1980s including Paul's other plays: *Breaking Up In Balwyn* (1983, on a riverboat), *Living Rooms* (1986, in an historic mansion) and *Full House/No Vacancies* (1989, in a boarding house). These works became the subject of his book *Really Moving Drama* (University of Queensland, 2013). Both *The Tram Show* and another play, *On Shifting Sandshoes* (1988) were awarded AWGIES, as was *Return of The Prodigal* (2000) an episode of *Something In The Air*. Paul has written two feature films *Neil Lynn* (with David Baker in 1984) and the Greater Union Award nominated *Exits* (1980). He has taught English Literature and Screenwriting at Southern Cross and James Cook Universities, as well as Melbourne State College, and conducted writing workshops and script consultancies for Screenworks Northern Rivers, and QPIX in Brisbane. His novel, *33 Postcards From Heaven* was published by Gondwana Press in 2005, and numerous articles, reviews, stories and interviews have been published in *Metro, Cinema Papers, Cantrill's Filmnotes, Australasian Drama Studies, Community Theatre In Australia, The Macquarie Companion to the Australian Media* and *Theatre Research International* (Cambridge University).

(24304)

www.ingramcontent.com/pod-product-compliance
Lightning Source LLC
Chambersburg PA
CBHW050317010526
44107CB00055B/2282